THE BOOK IN THE AGE OF THEATER
1550-1750

THE
BOOK
IN THE AGE OF
THEATER
1550-1750

LARRY F. NORMAN

with contributions by Joshua Phillips *and*

Véronique Sigu, Jeanne Tillman

& Delphine Zurfluh

THE UNIVERSITY OF CHICAGO LIBRARY 2001

1000 copies of this catalogue
were published in conjunction with an exhibition held in
the Department of Special Collections, University of Chicago Library
January 22, 2001–April 9, 2001.

Cover and section images reproduced from
Pierre Corneille. *Le Theatre*. Paris: Guillaume de Luyne, 1664.

Design and typesetting by Lynn Martin.
Photography by Ted Lacey.
Production editor Valarie Brocato.
Copy editor Britt Salvesen.
Printed by Universal Press.

Note: Full bibliographic information for works included
in the exhibition is provided in the *Checklist*. Several first editions cited
in the essays were represented by later editions.

Contributors to the catalogue:
LN Larry F. Norman
JP Joshua Phillips
VS Véronique Sigu
JT Jeanne Tillman
DZ Delphine Zurfluh

Library of Congress Cataloging-in-Publication Data
Norman, Larry F.
    The book in the age of theater, 1550-1750 / Larry F. Norman, with contributions by
Joshua Phillips and Véronique Sigu, Jeanne Tillman and Delphine Zurfluh.
        p. cm.
    ISBN 0-943056-27-6
    1. European drama--Bibliography--Exhibitions. 2. European drama--Early works to
1800--Exhibitions. 3. European drama--Illustrations--Exhibitions. 4. University of
Chicago. Library--Exhibitions.

Z5782.N67 2001
[PN1811]
809.2'0094--dc21   00-069625

CONTENTS

PREFACE

"The Book in the Age of Theater" considers the relationship between performance and print from 1550 to 1750, an era in which the audience and modern conventions for both plays and printed books were developing rapidly. The essays in this catalogue and the exhibition it accompanies examine the participation of printers, authors and actors, spectators and readers, patrons, censors and critics, in a network of interactions between "the stage" and "the page." Title pages, frontispieces and illustrations, prefaces and privileges, reveal tensions between the transitory oral and visual realm of theater and the presumably fixed printed page; while editions, translations, adaptations, criticism, and set design provide perspectives on the texts, contexts, and reception of the plays.

Traditional analytical bibliography has strong roots in the study of English Renaissance drama. The aim of reconstructing a work's production history from the physical evidence of the printed book was to establish accurate texts. More recently book historians have discovered that theater poses critical questions concerning the social and cultural aspects of printing, publishing, and reading; and theater historians have focused increased attention on similar issues surrounding the stage. Drawing on the theatrical holdings in the Department of Special Collections, "The Book in the Age of Theater" demonstrates the compatibility of these approaches: looking closely at the physical form and textual content of books illuminates the history of a literary genre and the experiences of its readers. The history of theater is a particular strength in Special Collections, reflecting the interest of early faculty members in both bibliographical research and studying the widest possible range of plays, from well known to obscure and even unpublished. Holdings include Italian Renaissance plays; the Celia and Delia Austrian Collection, principally of English Restoration drama; a collection of eighteenth-century French plays; the Morton and Beyer collections of American typescripts and playscripts from theatrical rental agencies; the Briggs Collection of drama reviews; and the Napier Wilt Index Collection documenting Chicago theater history.

Exhibitions afford opportunities to present and interpret collections, create new audiences, and bring visibility to distinctive resources. By creating opportunities for students and faculty to bring their specialized knowledge and purpose to the collections, they help to highlight comprehensive holdings and identify areas that need to be strengthened. In the course of this project, we marveled frequently at the seemingly never-ending versions of *Il Pastor fido*, but I will probably remember best the times that Larry Norman ever-so-gently questioned the lack of early Racine editions. This process plays an important role in collection development, and I am grateful for what we learned.

"The Book in the Age of Theater" was organized by Professor Larry F. Norman, Department of Romance Languages and Literatures, in conjunction with a seminar that also produced a Smart Museum exhibition, "The Theatrical Baroque." Four students in the seminar—Joshua Phillips, Véronique Sigu, Jeanne Tillman, and Delphine Zurfluh—each contributed essays and participated in selecting items for the exhibition. They were all enthusiastic about the materials and excited by the aesthetic and intellectual satisfactions of working with early printed books. Joshua Phillips took on the research and writing for several key topics, and his editorial efforts helped to blend the individual parts. Larry Norman guided the project with subtle skill and good humor, ensuring steady progress amidst the temptations to explore many choices and themes. His own introduction, a dramatic tour de force in its own right, exemplifies the insight, elegance, and wit he brought to the entire undertaking.

Several Special Collections staff members made important contributions to the project. Jay Satterfield and Debra Levine kept the supply of books flowing and prevented a flood. Deborah Derylak and Susanna Morrill prepared the check-list, carefully heeding the most intricate bibliographical details. Valarie Brocato skillfully organized, designed, and installed the exhibition, with assistance from Theresa Smith and Kerri Sancomb, and she oversaw production of the catalogue. It was a joy to work once again with Lynn Martin, who designed the catalogue with characteristic care and exquisite sensibility for the material.

ALICE SCHREYER
Curator of Special Collections

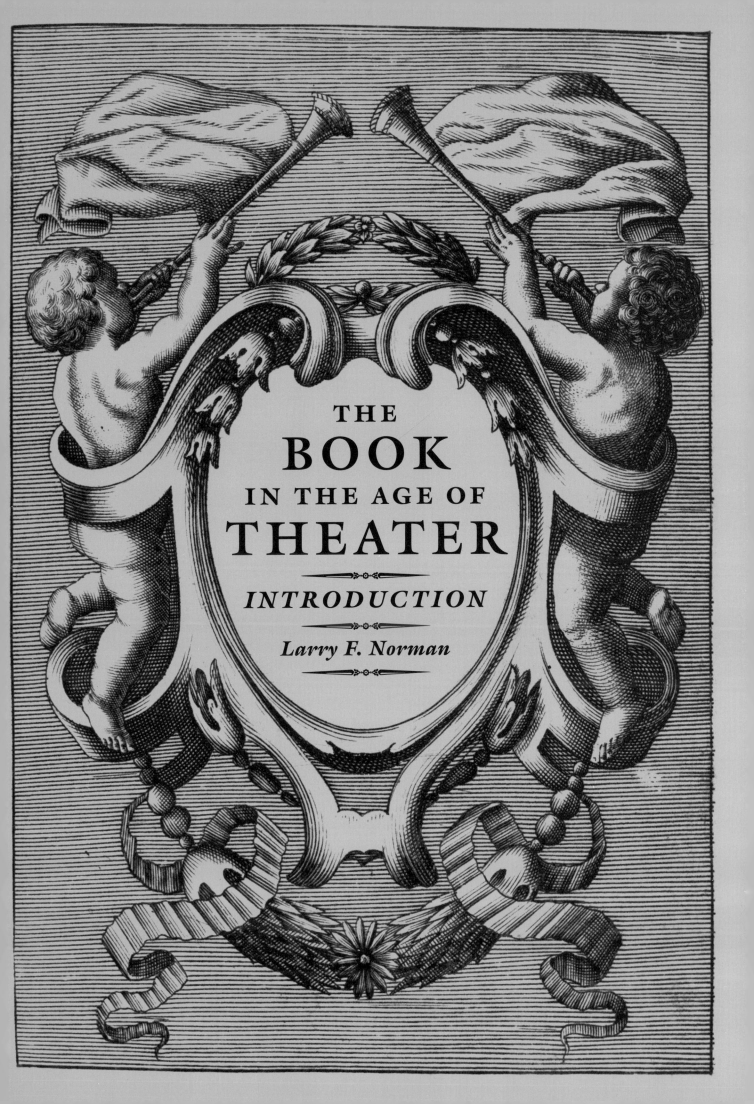

THE
BOOK
IN THE AGE OF
THEATER

INTRODUCTION

Larry F. Norman

INTRODUCTION

Imagine you are a reader secluded in the provinces of France during the 1630s. In your country retreat far from the baroque palaces, literary salons, and ambitious poets of Paris, you open a freshly printed play by the most promising young writer of the day, Pierre Corneille. While you may be most eager to read his new and wildly successful tragi-comedy, *Le Cid*—which has sparked a literary quarrel embroiling not only the just-founded Académie Française but even the prime minister, Cardinal Richelieu, himself—it is not Corneille's most recent play that you have in hand. It is instead his earlier comedy about current life in Paris, *La Galerie du palais*. The play, it is true, was first performed several years ago, but it has just now been published. Though this delay is somewhat unusual in length, a certain lagtime between performance and printing is quite typical in these years, as theatrical companies attempt to maximize playhouse revenues before letting commercial publication put the play into the hands of rival troupes. The playwright's newfound fame, however, has made publication of his earlier comedies a very timely venture.

If the book was sent by a Parisian friend, it might arrive with a letter reminiscing about the original stage production; the friend might even express regret—as would the great prose stylist Madame de Sévigné decades later when sending Racine's *Bajazet* to her distant daughter—that it was impossible to send the play's star performer along with the book, "for without this actress the piece loses half its merit." And the correspondent would have some reason for such a qualification: reading a French play at this time might appear at first glance quite an austere experience. In most cases, there were very few or simply no printed stage directions to inform the reader of the actors' movements. Though the past century had seen some innovative developments in this direction, in the seventeenth century, the French, like most of Europe, were still heavily influenced by the ancient Greek and Latin practice of recording only spoken lines. And even if there were some stage directions, they would most likely be limited to brief physical descriptions. Playwrights and editors made little effort to note expressive gestures, tone of voice, and interior emotional states; only later would the rising influence of the novel inspire such descriptive passages within dramatic texts. We are not yet in the reader-oriented world of Goethe's *Faust,* and Bernard Shaw's directorial chattiness is a universe away.

Faced then with what is largely a transcript of the spoken lines (with the principal design assistance of the act- and scene-divisions and notations of the characters on stage), you might naturally attempt to project before your eyes the staged performance and imagine yourself as a member of the Paris audience watching the production. After all, the theater was, then as now, primarily a visual experience. As France's leading theoretician of drama at the time, the Abbé d'Aubignac, noted, theatergoers are labeled "*spectators,* or *viewers,* and not *listeners;* and the place where these performances are held is called a *theater* and not an *auditorium,* that is to say, *a place where one watches what is done,* and not *where one listens to what is said.*" And effectively evoking this visual experience can be difficult work for the reader. Indeed it is such a demanding task that Molière would go so far as to suggest, in 1666, that only a special few are fit for it: "It is well known that plays are made only to be performed, and I do not advise the reading of [this play] to any but those who can imagine the entire theatrical performance based on a reading."

Molière's warning does not daunt our reader. You are, after all, far from the theater life of Town and Court and are accustomed to the imaginative challenge of seeing plays from between bookcovers. In the first act of the Corneille comedy, however, you encounter a curious scene that makes you question your own reading activity. The scene is set in the *galerie* of the title, a fashionable marketplace catering to the needs and wants of elite Parisians (figure 1). As the predictably rich, young, and beautiful characters of this romantic comedy pass among the shops retailing elegant clothing and accessories, they encounter another purveyor of luxury goods, the bookseller. And there is nothing accidental about his appearance here: the seamless congruity of fashion and publishing is dramatically illustrated in the dialogue, where the commercial language of a silk and lace *bou-*

Figure 1.   Abraham Bosse (1602-1676) "La Galeria du Palais" from André Blum, *Abraham Bosse* (1924)

tiquière rhythmically alternates with that of the bookseller. Indeed, the latter understands all too well that his business is feeding the public's interest in the latest trends of the Parisian world of letters. Thus when the romantic lead, Dorimant, enters and engages in a discussion about the new releases, the bookseller immediately provides an update on the latest literary fashion. And what's hot? Not novels, not gallant poetry, but comedies, tragedies, and tragi-comedies. "Theater plays are all the rage these days," reports the shopkeeper. As the characters proceed to bemoan the deluge of plays written by hack poets, Dorimant suggests that one playwright merits the praise of his interlocutor. And the playwright in question is none other than Corneille himself. "Your tastes, I know, are for Normandy," Dorimant quips, referring to the native region of the playwright who

Figure 2. Pierre Corneille, *The Cid: or, The Heroick Daughter. A Tragedy* (1714)

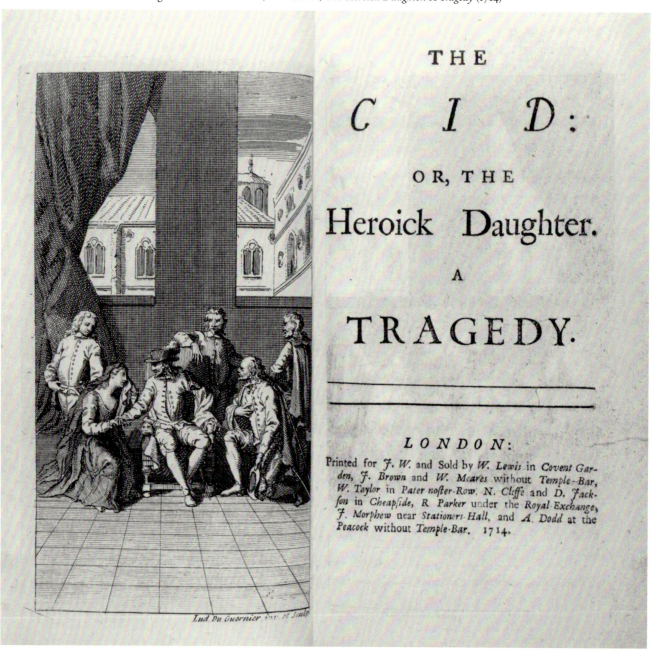

has not only written this scene but created his own character.

Corneille confected here a perfectly baroque turn of playful self-reference, much like the chapter of *Don Quixote* in which the hero hits upon the first volume of his own adventures. By the 1630s the French were used to finding plays in the bookshop, but to find a bookshop full of plays inside of a play proves a dizzying moment, especially since we are to understand that among the printed plays in the stage-set boutique are those of the playwright whose work is being performed. Or being read. To return to our imaginary provincial armchair, you are now reading a Corneille play about the kind of trendy Parisians who go to Corneille plays and who now consider buying one. Just as you are working at envisioning the play like a spectator, you enter a fictional bookshop and are instantly reminded that plays are printed

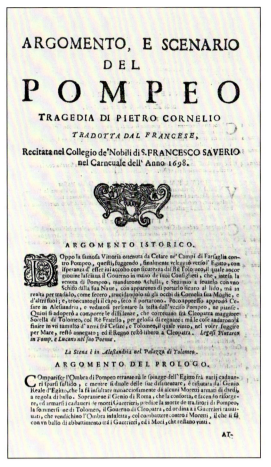

Figure 3. Pierre Corneille and
Thomas Corneille, *Tragedie* [1690-1700]

as well as performed, and that fashionable people like the characters in this play may now be reading this same play in Paris, and indeed, all over France. And soon all over Europe. In the years to come Corneille's early work will be republished many times, then collected in an authoritative volume; meanwhile, translations of his plays will nourish printers in England and fill performance spaces in Italy (figures 2 and 3). And just as each performance is in fact an interpretation, so too each new edition, translation, and adaptation—with their own physical formats and textual alterations—will transform the original and create fertile ground for new readings and new stagings.

The passage from *La Galerie* opens an elaborately baroque window onto the cultural landscape of the book in the age of theater—defined for our purposes as the period from the mid-sixteenth through the mid-eighteenth centuries—and also raises the most crucial questions that this exhibition addresses. But before introducing these key issues, let me briefly set the stage for the rich intellectual dialogue suggested by the bookseller scene. The printing press and the modern theater are both children of the Renaissance; they grew together and shaped each other in the course of the following centuries. But the printed book was born a century or so before the theater began its striking cultural ascent. Though Italian architects of the mid-sixteenth century built the first elaborately designed theaters since Antiquity, it was in the late sixteenth and early seventeenth centuries that drama became a dominant force throughout Western Europe. Whether in the Elizabethan and Jacobean England of Shakespeare and Jonson, in the Spanish Golden Age of Lope de Vega and Calderón, or in Richelieu's France, theater found itself protected by the powerful, patronized by the people, and theorized by the intellectuals. And though there were periods of difficulty, such as the closing of the playhouses in England under Cromwell, theater continued its triumph through the seventeenth century, reaching new peaks in Restoration England and Louis XIV's France, before seeing its glory eventually eclipsed by the rise of the novel in the eighteenth century.

What accounts for this spectacular success? It is of course always dangerous to wager on a simple cause and effect in cultural history, but all scholars would agree that two strong forces came together to help promote theater in the early modern period: the support of princely and royal courts, and the rise of a cultivated public enjoying the sociability of the playhouse as well as its artistic expressiveness. Both developments were associated with the decline of medieval feudalism, and the corresponding absorption of dispersed power by new centralized national courts. James I and Charles I of England, for example, understood perfectly how theater could reflect the glories of monarchy, and the results of their patronage include the sumptuous royal masques created by architect and stage designer Inigo Jones with poet Ben Jonson; these collaborative efforts effectively merged drama, dance, music, stage machinery, and sets to create a mirror of the court's splendors. Likewise, Cardinal Richelieu's effort to centralize the state and promote France's hegemony in Europe included a powerful drive to create what today we might call a national cultural policy, one that promoted theater as a motor for France's literary and artistic predominance. Meanwhile, the domestication of the former warrior class of the aristocracy created a new group of leisured nobles who increasingly sought distinction in their refined manners—and in their literary, artistic, and dramatic connoisseurship. This polite cultivation was in turn emulated by the rising bourgeoisie, its members often free from day-to-day business concerns and ready to join in the frivolity of playgoing—and to participate in the kind of conversational theater criticism practiced by the rich, leisured Parisians of *La Galerie du palais.*

But as the Corneille scene reminds us, the triumph of theater was also the triumph of the printed play—as well as the birth of theater journalism, as we will see. Successful as the alliance of print and drama was, however, the scene also helps us uncover the fascinating tensions and unique challenges that animate the dynamic exchange between theater and the book, tensions that are explored in the following catalogue essays and illustrated by the works in the exhibition.[1] These tensions and challenges arose primarily from the very special status of drama, from its profound association with individual live performances, with the idiosyncratic voices and gestures of actors, with the visual decor of the set, and, not least, with the palpable presence of (and potential interaction with) a crowd of spectators. How can this richly sensory experience possibly be translated in dry ink? To answer this question, the first part of this catalogue, "Performance and Printing," looks at the techniques used by playwrights and bookmakers to recreate performance conditions on the page. It was not uncommon, for example, for title pages to emphasize the place and time of the stage production, including the name of the acting company, to the exclusion of the playwright's name: the printed play was often viewed more as a product of a troupe's performance than the creation of a solitary author toiling with pen. And despite the absence or relative brevity of stage directions, some ingenious graphic devices were nevertheless invented to convey the movement and visuality of the theatrical experience.

But the bookseller scene makes clear that printed plays were more than mere autonomous transcripts of performance, however ingeniously designed. Printed plays existed in a larger universe made up of readers, playwrights, markets, and censors. The fashion-minded Dorimant's reference to Corneille's success reminds us that the book does not stand on literary merit alone, but is instead part of a energetic interaction among diverse audiences, political and ecclesiastic authorities, and career authors. And each of the social forces examined in the essays "The Power of Audiences," "Regulators and Censors," and "The Birth of the Playwright" not only intervenes in the production of the book but, more interestingly, also leaves its own highly visible, and often striking, mark on the book's pages. First the audience. Far from simply disappearing after the performance, the theater public often made a second appearance in print: its power as patron and consumer emerges in dedicatory letters and prefaces commenting on initial spectator reaction. Furthermore, title pages often boast about the constitution of the original audience; the standard line "As played before His Majesty at . . . ," for example, often competes with the name of the play for the reader's attention. At the other end of the artistic exchange, playwrights increasingly sought to leave their own mark on their printed works. Though we have seen that plays were frequently printed anonymously, seemingly attributed to the performing troupe, a number of authors attempted to take control of their own publication. As one might guess from his flattering self-reference in *La Galerie du palais,* Corneille was himself a pioneer in this effort, creating later in his career a handsome collected edition of his works that included self-promoting introductions to each play designed to mould readers' responses.

Producers and consumers were not the only agents shaping the printed play. Equally active, and sometimes highly negative, forces were those of Church and State. All officially sanctioned publications included what were the rough equivalents of copyright permissions, called "privileges," and these prose appendages sometimes went into some detail about the approval process for the work, even hazarding judgments on the play's merits. The censorship process, though, could make even more forceful interventions, including a total ban on the printing of a play, but it often worked in more subtle ways that left fascinating traces on the page for the attentive reader. Consider the example of Molière. Though the great

LE
TARTUFFE,
OU
L'IMPOSTEUR.
COMEDIE.

Par I. B. P. DE MOLIERE.

Les trois premiers Actes de cette Comedie
ont esté representez à Versailles pour le
Roy le 12. jour du mois de May 1664.

Les mesmes trois premiers Actes de cette
Comedie ont esté representez la deuxié-
me fois à Villers-Cotterests pour S. A. R.
MONSIEUR, Frere Unique du Roy,
qui regaloit leurs Majestez & toute la
Cour, le 25. Septembre de la mesme
année 1664.

A ij

Cette Comedie parfaite, entiere & achevée
en cinq Actes, a esté representée la premiere & la seconde fois au Chasteau du
Raincy, prés Paris, Pour S. A. S. Mon-
seigneur le Prince, les 29. Novembre 1664.
& 8. Novembre de l'année suivante 1665.
& depuis encor au Chasteau de Chantilly
le 20. Septembre 1668.

La premiere Representation en a esté donnée
au public dans la Salle du Palais Royal,
le 5. Aoust 1667. & le lendemain 6. elle
fut défenduë par Monsieur le Premier
President du Parlement jusques à nou-
vel ordre de Sa Majesté.

La permission de representer cette Comedie
en public sans interruption, a esté accor-
dée le 5. Février 1669. & dés ce mesme
jour la Piece fut representée par la Troupe
du Roy.

PREFACE.

OICY une Comedie dont on a fait
beaucoup de bruit, qui a esté long-
temps persecutée ; & les Gens
qu'elle joüe, ont bien fait voir qu'ils
estoient plus puissans en France que tous ceux
que j'ay joüez jusques icy. Les Marquis, les
Précieuses, les Cocus, & les Medecins, ont
souffert doucement qu'on les ait representez ; &
ils ont fait semblant de se divertir, avec tout le
monde, des peintures que l'on a faites d'eux :
Mais les Hypocrites, n'ont point entendu raille-
rie ; ils se sont effarouchez d'abord, & ont trou-
vé étrange que j'eusse la hardiesse de joüer leurs
grimaces, & de vouloir décrier un métier dont
tant d'honnestes Gens se meslent. C'est un cri-
me qu'ils ne sçauroient me pardonner, & ils se
sont tous armez contre ma Comedie avec une
fureur épouvantable. Ils n'ont eu garde de
l'attaquer par le costé qui les a blessez ; ils sont

A iij

TARTUFFE.

Je puis vous dissiper ces craintes ridicules,
Madame, & je sçay l'art de lever les scrupules.
Le Ciel défend, de vray, certains contentemens ;
  C'est un Scelerat qui parle.
Mais on trouve avec luy des accommodemens.
Selon divers besoins, il est une Science,
D'étendre les liens de nostre conscience,
Et de rectifier le mal de l'action
Avec la pureté de nostre intention.
De ces secrets, Madame, on sçaura vous instruire ;
Vous n'avez seulement qu'à vous laisser conduire.
Contentez mon desir, & n'ayez point d'effroy,
Je vous réponds de tout, & prens le mal sur moy.
Vous toussez fort, Madame.
  ELMIRE.

Figures 4, 5, 6, and 7.
Jean-Baptiste Molière, *Les Œuvres* (1697)

comic playwright was much loved by Louis XIV and the Paris theater public, he faced five years of continuous censorship (1664–69) for his masterful satire of religious hypocrisy, *Tartuffe*. And the story of the tortuous career of the play during the ban did not fade from the reader's attention in the years after. The 1697 edition, for example, recounts the story in elaborate detail, opening with a two-page timeline of the attempted performances and censors' actions during the ban. The timeline is followed by a preface by Molière arguing against the censors (figures 4,5,6). The effect of censorship is not limited to these supplementary introductions and timelines: it reshapes the very lines of the play itself. No doubt in order to mollify his critics, Molière had made some self-censoring revisions that could not but strike the 1697 reader. In an effort to safely distance himself from Tartuffe's scandalous attitudes, the playwright added to one of his character's impious speeches a parenthetical warning that "c'est un scélérat qui parle" ("it's a villain speaking") (figure 7). This note to the reader is all the more conspicuous given that Molière, like almost all playwrights of the time, rarely provided any stage directions describing his characters' personality or attitudes. And this was not the only case in which censorship altered the printed version of a Molière play. When his long banned *Dom Juan* was finally printed posthumously in 1682, the French editors cut a number of irreligious lines that were fortunately preserved in the more daring Dutch edition of the following year. One such censored line features the ridiculously pious servant, Sganarelle, revealing his hypocrisy at the end of the play. As his libertine master is dragged to hell, presumably with his moneypurse in hand, the surprised Sganarelle abandons his usual moralizing posture and screams a desperate last plea of "mes gages, mes gages!" ("hey, my salary!"). In this case, meaning—and laughter—depend on the edition you read.

Both the censor's hand and the playwright's revisions suggest just how malleable the printed play could be. But posterity also leaves its marks. While neglect may safely fix an original edition, fame assures a life full of surprising textual twists and turns. The essays "Editions and Transformations" and "Crossing Borders" track some of the profound metamorphoses experienced by successful plays as they passed among publishers, translators, and adapters. Shakespeare's plays, for example, were frequently "improved" in the seventeenth century in order to make them more seemly to polite Restoration audiences; *King Lear* even found itself blessed with a happy ending by adapter Nahum Tate. And though Shakespeare long remained ignored in France, when he did finally reach some popular attention in the 1730s, through a moderately appreciative essay by Voltaire, the politely condescending *philosophe* proffered only the highly altered translations of a few detached monologues.

Of course, when a work passes into another author's hand, kind results should not necessarily be expected. Adaptation is often literary rivalry disguised as homage. But there are yet crueler forms of literary appropriation than adaptation, and the dramatic parodists surveyed in "Crossing Genres" reveal just how ruthless staged lampoons of high drama could be in the hands of popular theater troupes.

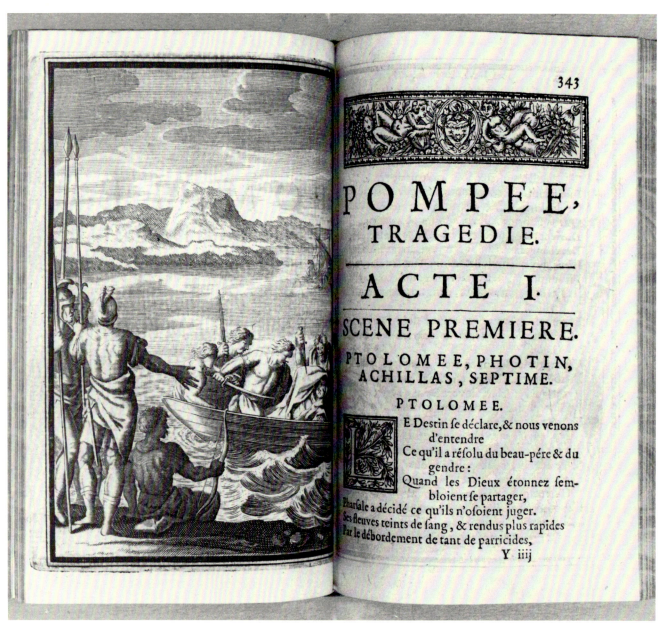

Figure 8. Pierre Corneille, *Le theatre* (1664)

In the early eighteenth century, for example, the inheritors of French farce and Italian *commedia dell'arte* crafted keen satires of masterpieces by playwrights from Sophocles to Voltaire, while simultaneously throwing themselves into the literary and professional quarrels animating the theater world of their own day. Elaborately self-reflexive as these satires may be, there is nothing surprising about this kind of theatrical introspection. As Corneille's bookseller scene so well demonstrates, when "theater plays are all the rage," the stage itself follows the fashion—and plays often become plays about plays. The theater world turns its gaze upon itself, and not just in the form of burlesque parodies. In a more realistic vein, Molière took the kind of polite cultivated conversation about literary fashions evoked in *La Galerie du palais* and created an entire play, the 1663 *Critique de l'Ecole des femmes,* that consists solely of leisured Parisians in a salon discussing his own latest play, *L'Ecole des femmes.* As might be assumed, Molière was hardly impartial in his depiction, roundly mocking the critics of the title for their attacks on his earlier play.

Naturally, this widespread obsession with theater could hardly be limited solely to the terrain of dramatic dialogue. It richly expressed itself as well in the emerging genres of drama criticism and journalism that are probed in the second part of this exhibition. The elaborate theories concerning drama concocted by Renaissance scholars soon became popularized by theatrical quarrels that consumed cultivated conversation throughout Europe. Indeed, the Abbé d'Aubignac reported that in mid-seventeenth century Paris "there is not a single salon where women do not undertake to give lessons" about various rules and guidelines for good drama. Playwrights like Lope de Vega, John Dryden, and, of course, Corneille weighed in with essays directed to their audiences. And as periodicals began to develop in the decades thereafter, popular interest in plays, whether newly staged or freshly printed, nourished their pages and fed their sales.

But for all this talk about drama, talk alone cannot tell the whole story of the theatrical experience. Plays are made up of dialogue, certainly, but d'Aubignac was correct to insist that playgoers are above all "spectators" and not "listeners." Fortunately, however, the book's expressiveness is not confined to the textual. It also employs a powerful arsenal of visual devises, the most potent of which was then the engraved image. The section "Illustrating Theater" evokes the brilliant splendors born of the encounter between stage and page. It reminds us that the opulence of the play is not just in its performance, however well acted and staged

it may have been, but also in the space where that performance took place. From the revival of Vitruvian architecture through the riches of the rococo, theater buildings served to ornament not only the cities of Europe, but also the sumptuously illustrated pages of luxury books. Likewise, the grandeur of theatrical spectacles staged in royal courts, vast formal gardens, and public piazzas were frequently committed to print in deluxe engravings commemorating the events.

Book illustrations were not limited to architectural glories and resplendent theatrical festivities. In the form of frontispieces, they also serve to fuel the imagination of the reader opening up a humble dramatic text. A final return to our provincial seventeenth-century

Figure 9. Pierre Corneille, *Le Theatre* (1664)

armchair, though, shows that not all plays were blessed with this kind of visual aid. In the mid-1630s the engraved frontispiece was a luxury not yet easily granted to a Corneille play. But as the playwright's stature grew in the coming years, all of his works would be adorned with frontispiece illustrations (including later editions of *La Galerie du palais*). These frontispieces picture for the reader thrilling scenes of duels on land, assassinations at sea, and idol-smashing in the temple (figure 8). What is perhaps most fascinating about these fiercely graphic images is that they illustrate scenes that were never actually staged. The rules of decorum governing French theater at the time forbade any such physical violence before the eyes of spectators; the actions depicted thus took place off stage and were relayed to the audience only by the narrations of entering messengers. But for those first confronting the play in printed form, these scenes must have seemed just as visually striking as those that were actually performed. The reader's imagination, after all, is as likely to be fueled by a beautifully rendered verbal evocation of a duel from the mouth of a messenger as by a scene of dialogue with little or no stage directions. No doubt the splendid baroque depictions featured in these frontispieces give us a glimpse into the visual repertory of a seventeenth-century reader's imagination. If so, we might surmise that even in an age of fabulous stage machinery, sumptuous decors, and moving declamatory performances, no single theater stage could ever equal the one that is magically raised before the reader's armchair.

1. For an excellent introduction to the relation between book history and theater in the period, see Roger Chartier's *Publishing Drama in Early Modern Europe* (London: The British Library, 1999). Chartier has been a pioneer in this field and we are indebted to his work for the present exhibition and catalogue.

PROLOGUE

HUMANISM

Joshua Phillips

PROLOGUE
HUMANISM

Although theatrical performances of many varieties—mystery plays, city pageants, court spectacles—were quite common throughout medieval and Renaissance Europe, the earliest printers did not instinctively emphasize the drama as a source for their trade. Theater presented many aspects that must have seemed anathema to printing: it was often highly localized, spontaneous, collective, and frequently tied to specific occasions, such as religious days and feasts. Fortunately, however, in the fifteenth century and following, many publishers and the people who worked with them were trained as humanists; thus they were inclined to edit and reprint Latin and Greek classics as part of their goal of emulating and surpassing classical culture. In Italy, the home of humanism, much care and attention were given to Plautus, Terence, and Seneca, the only Latin dramatists whose works survived. One early edition—*Plautus integer cum interpretatione* (1500)—shows the care and scholarship with which such documents were treated. But it also shows how such drama was meant to be approached: as an object of study and literary veneration, not as something to be acted. The extensive commentary surrounding the text of the play, which resembles medieval manuscript glosses, hardly allows for a direct reading of the play itself. An early collection of plays by Terence even includes an illustration depicting the works being read rather than performed. Other less scholarly formats, however, quickly became available. The edition *M. Plauti Sarssinatis Comedie* (1513) provides "arguments" before each play, but presents little commentary, and its small, packed format would not even provide room for a reader's notes.

Terence, *P Terentii Aphri Comico[rum] elegantissimi comedie* (1505)

Greek plays in the original were clearly directed at a specialized audience and could only be produced by printers who knew (or had editors who knew) the language

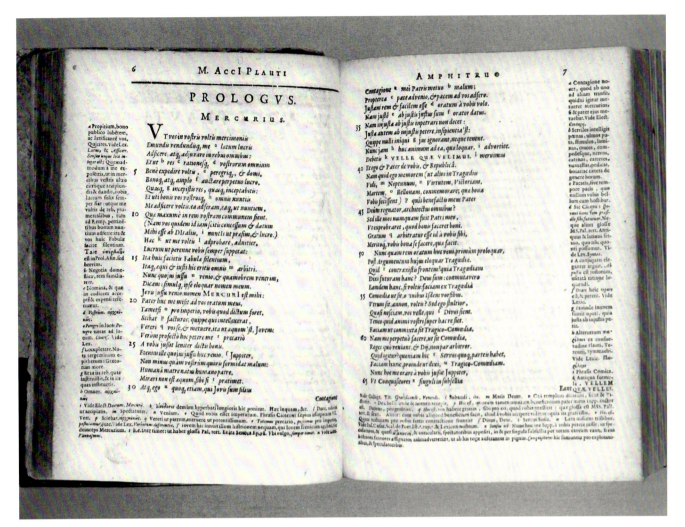

Plautus, *Comoediæ XX* (1619)

and who had the necessary Greek characters. Aldus Manutius was one such printer; he was praised by Erasmus for creating a "library" through his printing "that has no other limits than the world itself." His production of *Sophoclis tragædiæ septem cum commentariis* (1502) must have been a great gift to scholars of Greek; these plays, however, could only have been performed by and for an extremely elite, educated group. However, soon after the publication of the original texts, translations and vernacular imitations such as Trissino's *La Sophonisba* (1524)—one of the first Italian plays modeled on Sophoclean tragedy—began to appear in print and on stage.

The work of these early humanists (and not only in Italy) had two major consequences. First, it established a scholarly tradition that would allow for new erudite editions, very soon in vernacular languages, to be produced and published. Examples include an Italian version of *Oedipus Rex* (1565), a bilingual Latin/Spanish edition of Terence in 1583, and a new edition of Plautus in Paris in 1619, replete with marginal notes and commentary. Second, the publication of these plays inspired a vast number of playwrights to try to surpass the ancients. Perhaps because of the large number of extant plays by Plautus and Terence, coupled with a native comic tradition, hundreds of Italian authors turned to playwriting in the first half of the sixteenth century, with the bulk trying their hand at varieties of the New Comedy. These Italian authors inspired by the Classics would, in turn, exert an influence on other playwrights such as Shakespeare (as in his *Comedy of Errors*) and Molière (as in *L'Avare*). As time went on, tragedy and pastoral also became very popular. By 1750 more than six thousand plays had been printed in Italy alone.

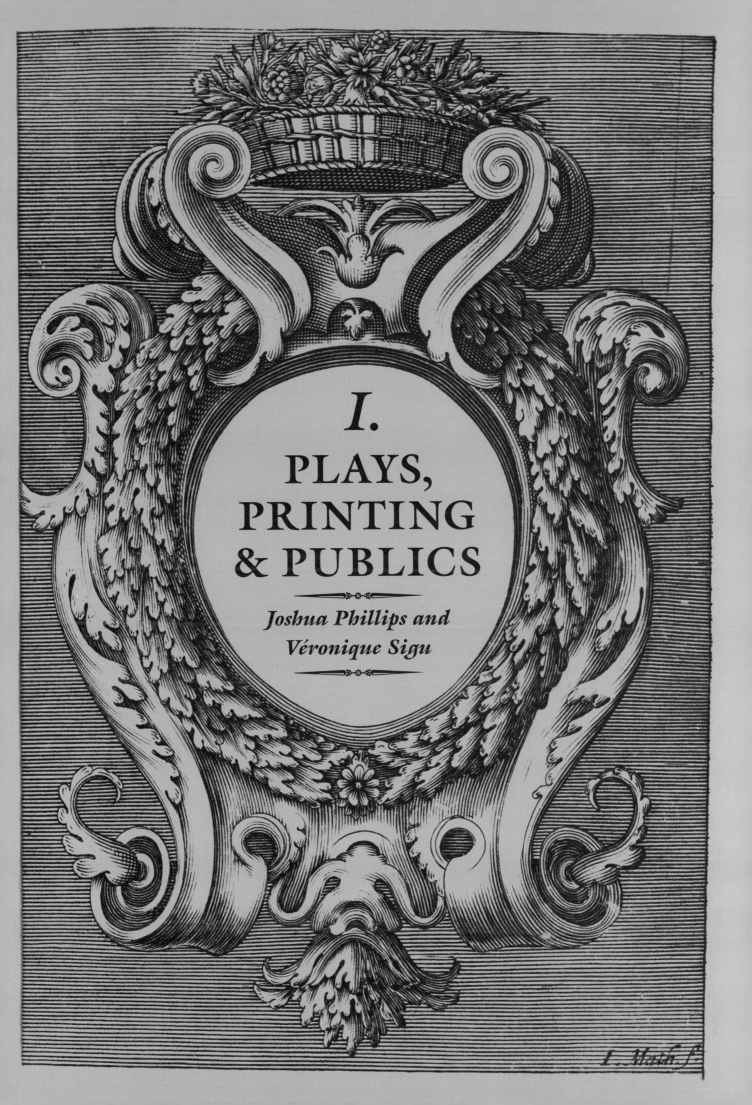

I.
PLAYS, PRINTING & PUBLICS

Joshua Phillips and
Véronique Sigu

PLAYS, PRINTING AND PUBLICS

Performance & Printing

Insofar as the first printed dramas, with a few notable exceptions, were generally objects of study and reading, one might say that the "printed drama" was born as a literary rather than performative art. That changed quickly, however, as printers started producing contemporary plays. In fact, by the late sixteenth century, reports of the success of a performance could be used to persuade readers that the printed play would be equally enjoyable. But some printers and authors were not so confident that successful performances would inevitably translate into quality literature. Many authors claimed to be uneasy about or even disgusted by having their works in print. In the first half of the sixteenth century, the actor and playwright Angelo Beolco (known as Ruzzante) pointed to the great discrepancy he saw between literary and performative art, stating "Molte cose stanno ben nella penna che nella scena starebbon male" ("Many things work well from the pen which work badly on the stage"). In mid-seventeenth-century England, John Marston claimed that it "afflicts me, to thinke that Scænes invented, meerely to be Spoken, should be inforcively published to be read."

At nearly the same time in France, M. de Scudéry wondered whether the approbation his play had received in the theaters was truly "un effect de ses beautez" or rather of "le superbe appareil de la Scene, la face du Theatre, qui change cinq ou six fois entierement, à la representation de ce Poeme, la magnificence des habits, l'excellence des Comediens, de qui l'action farde les paroles, & la voix qui n'est qu'un son qui meurt en naissant" ("the superb trappings of the Stage, the face of the Theater, which changes entirely five or six times during the representation of this Poem, the magnificence of the costumes, the excellence of the actors, whose actions embellish the words, and the voice which is simply a sound that dies as it is being born"). If the visual and performative aspects were what had impressed the audience, Scudéry worried that a printed version might not achieve, or merit, success. Printers attempted to use their own extratextual visual material, such as large clear type and elegant frontispieces, to add to the beauties of the printed text. The printer of Scudéry's own *Mort de Cæsar,* for example, included a handsome frontispiece that—through its depictions of columns, spectators in the foreground, and a centered and raised visual focus—emphasizes the theatrical element of historical events.

In the shadow of the performance/print divide, however, two traditions,

Within the illustration:

SPQR.

SPQR

La Mort
de Cæsar.
Tragedie.
Par Monſ. de Scuderÿ

Auec Priuilege du Roy. 1636.

Miehvan lochom fecit

VRNE

A. PARIS,
Chez A. Courbé, Libraire, et Impr. de Monſeigr. frère du Roy, au Palais, en la petite ſalle, a la Palme.

M. (Georges) de Scudéry, *La Mort de Cæsar, tragedie* (1637) which maintained some autonomy, persisted. On the one hand, popular and improvisational theater continued to resist publication. Although we have many documents related to the *commedia dell'arte*, for example, we have few printed scripts or transcriptions of what was actually spoken onstage during these performances. On the other hand, texts in Latin and Greek with little hope of performance (except sometimes in academic contexts) continued to be printed regularly, as did certain other forms, such as Alexandre Hardy's verse-drama adaptation of Heliodorus' *Ethiopica*, which appears to have been written, unlike much of Hardy's huge œuvre, specifically for reading rather than viewing. Even the vastly popular *Pastor fido* was often seen as a delight for readers rather than spectators; it was printed *prior* to being represented on stage, and in the seventeenth century, the play's French translator claimed that because its plot was so familiar, "aussi est-elle plus du Cabinet que du Theatre, & plus propre pour estre leuë, que pour estre representée" ("it is therefore better suited to the study than to the Theater, and more proper to be read than to be acted"). Very often, however, successful performances did coincide with successful printed plays, and printers could gloat, as William Leake did on the title page of Beaumont and Fletcher's *Philaster*, that the play, "approved by the seeing Auditors, or Hearing Spectators (of which sort I take or conceive you to be the greatest part) hath received (as appears by the copious vent of four Editions), no less acceptance with improvement of you, likewise the Readers." The printer used the verso of the title page to advertise other plays and books he had printed.

There were also specific attempts to bridge the gap between performance and reading. One of the important means of diminishing the differences was the inclusion of stage directions. Classical theater almost entirely lacks such indications—there are only fourteen instances of what might be considered "stage directions" in all extant ancient Greek drama and not many more in Latin plays. The ancients, especially the Greeks, tended to indicate action through the speech of characters. Recently scholars have proposed, therefore, that stage directions stem from the popular theater of the middle ages, which was more centered on presenting action than rhetoric. Perhaps the most famous of all early English stage directions comes from the third act of Shakespeare's *Winter's Tale*, in which Antigonus is instructed to "Exit, pursued by a bear." One can only bemusedly wonder exactly what this stage direction was supposed to do: would the director have dressed a man as a bear to chase Antigonus? Or was it a note to the reading audience? In the absence of manuscript prompt-books or other materials, it is difficult to know whether stage directions were used to inform actors and directors of how things were to be done, or whether they were added by authors and printers to help the reader understand what took place onstage. Sometimes authors, especially those who were conscious of their reading (as well as their spectating) audience, would include stage directions that seem specifically intended for readers, such as Ben Jonson's note in *The Divell is an Asse* that one of the characters "expresses a longing to see the Divell." On the other hand, Chapman's note, in his

De Chapoton, *Le veritable Coriolan, Tragedie* (1638)

Revenge of Bussy D'Ambois, "Music, and the G[h]ost of Bussy enters" seems designed to inform potential directors of the play to provide music at this point.

Stage directions were not the only way that writers and printers attempted to reach out to their reading audiences. Lists of *dramatis personae*, sometimes with the names of both the characters and the actors, may have helped readers to visualize what happened onstage. Also, "arguments" that explain the context of the play (and that were sometimes spoken onstage as "Prologues") and marginal notes giving not only stage directions but also information about the scene, character, or history all helped readers to gather what, in a performance, would have been conveyed by gesture, costume, staging, and scenery. Pierre Larivey, in his collected *Comedies facesieuses . . . à l'imitation des anciens Grecs, Latins, & modernes Italiens* (1597), attempted to express through a complicated typographical process that different people were speaking at the same time. His particular attempt to bring the temporality and vitality of the stage to the page was not very successful, but printers continued to seek ways to make the action more accessible to readers.

Throughout the sixteenth and seventeenth centuries, the first thing that a consumer of a printed play was likely to see, even before purchasing it, was the title page. In the stalls where booksellers hawked their wares, these merchants would hang copies of the title pages of the works they were selling. Attractive printer's emblems and large type could be used to attract the buyer's attention. Sometimes an illustration depicting a scene from or referring to the play itself would adorn the title page, as for example on Middleton and Rowley's *A Faire Quarrell.* That title page also illustrates one of the more common ways that printers, especially in England, connected the printed versions of the plays with the performances of them. It states that *A Faire Quarrell* was "Acted before the King and divers times publikely by the Prince his Highnes Servants." Printers emphasized the esteemed audience before whom a work was played or the reputable theater in which it was performed to suggest that a work that had been "played to great applause" would be equally worthy of approbation from its readers. Although this practice was perhaps most common in England, it is not unusual to find a French play, such as de Chapoton's *Le Veritable Coriolan,* announcing both on the title page and on the frontispiece that it had been "representée par la Troupe Royale." Re-editions would even tout performances that had taken place decades earlier. The title page to a 1633 edition of John Lyly's *Gallathea* declares with the utmost precision that it was "played before the Queenes Maiestie at Greenwich, on New-yeeres Day at Night By the Children of Pauls"; it fails to mention, however, that the performance took place in front of Queen *Elizabeth* over thirty years earlier. This convention was so established in England by the mid-seventeenth century that the publisher of Thomas Nabbes's *The Unfortunate Mother* (1640) deemed it appropriate to signal that the play was "Never acted; but set downe according to the intention of the author." And the author himself lamented that his play, which an acting troupe had refused to perform, "hath beene denied the credit which it might have gained from the stage." These comments indicate that in the minds of many printers and readers, credit accrued to a published play from the reception it had as a performance. By the later seventeenth century indications of the first performance of a play, especially one by a well-known playwright, often seem designed merely to record a historical fact rather than to advertise. In *Les Œuvres de Molière* (1697), for example, the printer's note that *L'Avare* was "representée pour la premiere fois à Paris, sur le Theatre du Palais Royal, le 9. du mois de Septembre 1668" appears more a factual note than an attempt to persuade. –J.P.

The Power of Audiences

While many of the first readers of printed drama were humanist scholars, translations into vernacular languages, followed by the production of a wide variety of new plays, greatly expanded the audience for plays. Pope Leo X (1475–1521) loved the theater and supported its development as would Queen Elizabeth of England (1533–1603) and Cardinal Richelieu (1585–1642) and Louis XIV of France (1638–1715). Throughout the sixteenth and seventeenth centuries, theatrical performances were played in courts and palaces across Europe. The large number of dedications to aristocratic patrons does not prove that the dedicatees saw the plays performed or appreciated these texts, but the voluminous evidence of plays, masques, and royal spectacles performed before kings and dukes—sometimes with these nobles involved in the performances themselves—does speak to a love of drama. James Shirley's masque *The Triumph of Peace* (1633) indicates that it was performed by gentlemen "before the King and Queenes Majesties," and Molière's comedy *Les Plaisirs de l'isle enchantée* was "meslée de Danse & de Musique . . . & autres Festes galantes & magnifiques, faites par le Roy."

Indeed, no one did more to patronize the theater than Louis XIV and his court. The rise of the French opera provides a perfect example of royal engagement in the arts. The text of the privilege to the 1686 edition of Quinault's opera *Bellérophon* explicitly situates the piece in the context of royal protection, noting that Louis XIV created the Académie de Musique with the specific intention of developing a French lyrical drama, a "pièce de théâtre chantée," that would surpass its Italian sources. However, productions such as Quinault's *Opéras du Roy* are not the only instances of such royal patronage. In addition to the numerous court productions of comedies, tragedies, and ballets, the mere entrance of the king—*entrée royale*—in a city would occasion a grand spectacle such as the one depicted in Claude-François Menestrier's *L'Autel de Lyon*. The Court, of course, was not alone in patronizing theater in France's Ancien Régime. Convents and colleges often adapted or created plays acted by aristocratic or elite children; however, the power of royalty remained active even here, as is demonstrated by the 1747 print-

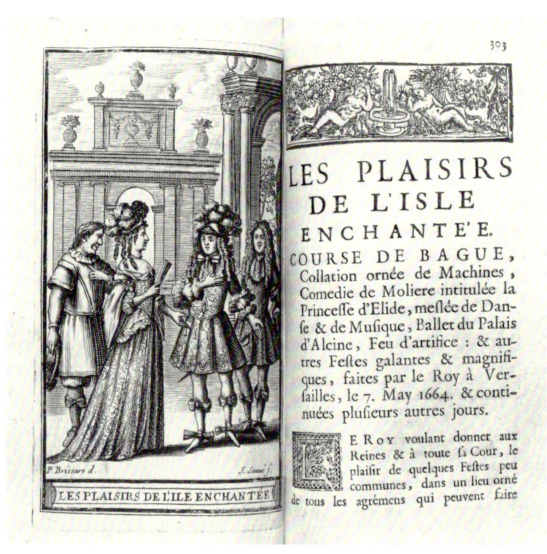

303

LES PLAISIRS DE L'ISLE ENCHANTE'E. COURSE DE BAGUE, Collation ornée de Machines, Comedie de Moliere intitulée la Princesse d'Elide, meslée de Danse & de Musique, Ballet du Palais d'Alcine, Feu d'artifice : & autres Festes galantes & magnifiques, faites par le Roy à Versailles, le 7. May 1664. & continuées plusieurs autres jours.

LE Roy voulant donner aux Reines & à toute sa Cour, le plaisir de quelques Festes peu communes, dans un lieu orné de tous les agrémens qui peuvent faire

Jean-Baptiste Molière, *Les Œuvres* (1697)

ing of *Les Incommodités de la grandeur*, played at the prestigious institution named in praise of Louis XIV, the "College Louis Le Grand."

No doubt this courtly proclivity for drama was related to the fact that the function of royalty was itself largely performative. In fact at the time of his death, Charles I's 1649 execution was described as a final masque. We know less about whether members of the royalty and aristocracy were also reading printed drama. However, the personal addresses in the texts speak to the authors' hopes that they were. For example, in the letter with which Pierre Le Hayer du Perron prefaced his play *Les Heureuses Advantures* (1633), he quite simply asked for a job: "Si vous me faisiez l'honneur de m'employer, vous remarqueriez assurément que je sçaurois de meilleure grace exposer ma vie & mon bien pour vostre service que faire des vers" ("If you would do me the honor of employing me, you would surely see that I know how to expose my life and goods with better grace than in writing verses"). Furthermore, the continued production of expensive folios, very often with profusely thankful dedications to specific individuals, indicates the importance of patronage and authors' efforts to stimulate sales by aristocratic associa-

-32--32-

tion. Nonetheless, it is certain that the majority of consumers of printed drama were not aristocrats. The texts themselves, like so many of the non-dramatic texts of this period, address the problem of this heterogeneous audience both through dedications to individual patrons and epistles to the generic "reader." Beaumont and Fletcher's comedy *The Knight of the Burning Pestle* begins with an impudent grocer demanding that the play be changed to suit his tastes. And *Hans Beer-Pot*, by (the aptly named, or pseudonymous) Daubridgcourt Belchier, advertises on its title page that it was acted by "an honest company of health-drinkers" and was clearly intended for an audience of the same. In Spain the prolific playwright Lope de Vega even wrote an "art of the play which is today acceptable to the taste of the crowd . . . for since the crowd pays for the comedies, it is fitting to talk foolishly to it to satisfy its taste." Concrete evidence also resides in the texts themselves. Folios, usually reserved for collected works, were costly, and individual plays were much more likely to be found in cheaper octavo and quarto formats. Very often printers condensed as much material as possible into the smallest number of pages. These texts were not intended for acting, studying, or display; they were simply meant to be sold cheaply and read. However, the intersection of writing, performance, and print varied considerably. Printed programs included with a manuscript version of the Italian translations of Corneille (1690–1700) inform the reader that a number of the most significant nobles of Bologna performed these plays during the pre-Lenten festivities of the *Carnevale;* the translations themselves, however, were never published. –J.P.

Regulators & Censors

Today, the Inquisition and infamous *Index librorum prohibitorum* cast their long shadows over the whole of the Renaissance. However, it is important to remember that official control over publishing was not always simply restrictive. While there is a good deal of overlap, it is useful to distinguish between official approval of a printing enterprise, in the form of privileges and patents that granted a commercial monopoly for a work, and governmental or ecclesiastic censorship. Censorship was used by governments and religious authorities to regulate and restrict what could be expressed and communicated; it could affect either the printing or performance of drama. Privileges were granted to printers as a means of regulating economic affairs within the printing industry and often approximated a copyright system. Whereas censorship tended to limit what got published or performed, privileges often worked to create an economic environment that made printing profitable, thereby providing an incentive to printers and publishers. In early modern Europe, however, both privileges and censorship were notoriously difficult to enforce, especially outside of any given territory.

The earliest printing privilege appears to have been granted in the Republic of Venice in 1469. Within the next half century, all the major European powers (and most of the minor ones) would institute some sort of privilege system. The form of these privileges, as well as their duration, the penalties for infringement, and the type of governing body awarding them changed over time and varied from country to country and even from region to region. When Scarron's *Le Jodelet* was published, in 1645, by Toussainct Quinet, it bore a five-year privilege, which was printed with the play and listed the punishments for contravening it; when *Le Jodelet* was printed by Antoine Ferrand in 1654, it appeared without any reference at all to a privilege. If, as it appears, Quinet did not renew his privilege, the text must have fallen into the "public domain" and then been legally reprinted by Ferrand. Meanwhile, in England, Queen Mary had granted a charter to the Stationers' Company (the guild that comprised printers, bookbinders, and book-sellers) in 1557. As a result of this document, stationers could simply pay a fee to register for the rights to a certain text, which meant no other stationer could print that work. This process was separate from that of licensing or approving the contents of books, and, because all registrations were recorded by the company, it was not necessary to print the privilege on the plays themselves. Protecting rights in copies across borders was almost impossible; a book printed in Paris, for example, could be reprinted without any fear of penalty in Geneva.

Censorship in the sixteenth and seventeenth centuries was even more protean. Even before Luther made his claim that printing was "God's highest and extremest act of grace, whereby the business of the Gospel is driven forward," the Catholic Church had grown wary of its powers. In 1515 Pope Leo X declared that all texts in Christendom would have to undergo prepublication censorship; this was followed, half a century later, by the creation of the *Index librorum prohibitorum*. Plays from this period still bear the traces of that institution. Boldoni's *L'Annuntiata* of 1636, for example, announces that it had been seen and approved by the Inquisitor's office. Yet even the most Catholic of monarchs tended to resist papal encroachments on their sovereign power, while trying to minimize incendiary material. In 1548 the Parlement of Paris prohibited religious plays and performances, but enforcement was inconsistent at best; by the early seventeenth century, even the best-known playwrights in France were writing religious dramas, although they were sometimes severely criticized for doing so. In England, Queen Elizabeth disallowed plays with religious subject matter from being performed. But outright prohibition on entire categories of plays was not the only means of censorship. In most places printed plays—like any other printed material—were read and authorized by some governmental or ecclesiastic authority. In Spain regulation was especially strict; every new play had to be examined and, in some cases, "edited" by the monarch's or Protector's appointee, and police were empowered to survey and close performances, if necessary. In England performances of plays were authorized by the Master of the Revels, while printed versions had to go through the normal procedures of licensing, which by the early seventeenth century was the responsibility of the archbishops of London and Canterbury. The printed version of one of William D'Avenant's plays collapsed the two processes; its title page carries the notice that "*The Witts*, as it was Acted without offence, may bee Printed not otherwise. 19. January 1635," signed by the Master of the Revels. That "not otherwise" also allows us to take this edition of *The Witts* as one of the few printed texts of Renaissance England that most likely presents the play as it was performed.

Censorship was in no way reserved for minor playwrights. Aside from the indirect coercive influence it exerted, censorship—in the form of punishment or threats—directly touched important playwrights such as Ben Jonson, who was briefly imprisoned for his collaboration in the play *The Isle of Dogs* and was called before the Privy Council on suspicion of treason for his *Sejanus*. And as Molière's case proves (see "Introduction," p. 15), censorship worked in strange and extremely uneven ways. It could not be enforced across territorial boundaries (as the more daring edition of *Dom Juan* published in Amsterdam shows), and it was applied inconsistently and sometimes capriciously by individual rulers. Middleton's *Game at Chess,* for example, which quite explicitly criticizes the king's Spanish policy, was allowed to play for nine straight days before being closed under the pressure

Giovanni Nicolò Boldoni, *L'Annunitiata* (1636)

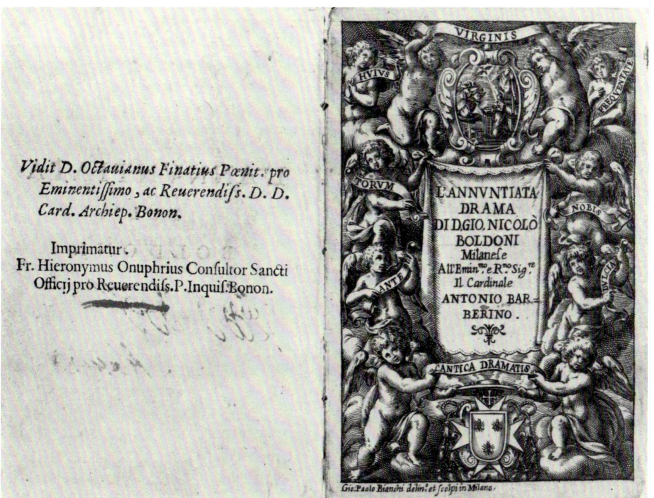

Thomas Middleton, *A Game at Chess* [1625?]

of the Spanish ambassador. It was, however, published and made widely available soon thereafter. And one of the most notable instances of censorship in Stuart England silenced not the theater, but an anti-theater critic. In 1633 William Prynne had both his ears cut off and his violently anti-theater work, *Histrio-mastix,* prohibited when Queen Henrietta Maria took offense at a slightly veiled slur aimed at her. But nine years later, with the advent of the Civil War in England, Prynne's side emerged victorious and the Puritans closed the theaters. Plays continued to be printed, however, and the printed book thus became the only medium for "experiencing" theater. –J.P.

The Birth of the Playwright

The sixteenth and seventeenth centuries were critical in the development of a modern concept of authorship. In Italy, where Dante, Bocaccio, and Petrarch dominated the literary imagination, the practice of highlighting the names of individual writers occurred much earlier than elsewhere. Already in the early 1500s, one finds the names of authors grandly displayed on Italian title pages: Ariosto (whose portrait is presented in the frontispiece to *Cassaria*), Machiavelli, Bibbiena, Trissino, and numerous others. The tension between the desire to emulate the ancients and to produce something new and different can be seen in Bibbiena's preface to his *Calandra,* in which he declared that his play is "in prosa, non in versi, moderna, non antica, volgare, non latina" ("in prose, not in verse; modern, not antique; vernacular, not Latin") and warned those who look for Plautus or Terence in it that they would search in vain. In France and especially in England, authorial attribution remained far less important for quite some time. Part of the reason must have been the collaborative nature of theater. Directors, actors, and printers all helped to shape plays, which were often composed by multiple writers in the first place. In France one could find a play, entitled *L'Aveugle de Smyrne* (1638), whose only attribution is to "les cinq auteurs" (a group convoked by Richelieu), even though one of the anonymous five was Pierre Corneille. And throughout Europe scores of unattributed or misattributed plays were printed every year. Even the very handsome edition of Corneille's *Le Menteur* (1644) omits the author's name from the title page, only providing it at the bottom of a prefatory letter addressed "à Monsieur." In England the situation was similar. A number of Shakespeare's plays, for example, were first printed entirely without attribution. And in 1640 a letter from "The Printer and The Stationer" prefaced to *A Mad World, My Masters* assured the reader that the author's "knowne Abilities will survive to all Posterities"; however, they failed to mention on the title page the name of that great author, Thomas Middleton.

One of the reasons for this authorial neglect was the complex and still

Lodovico Ariosto, *Comedia* (1536)

inchoate sense of who controlled or "owned" the play-text. Most often during the sixteenth and early seventeenth centuries, it belonged to the acting company; however, when the troupe sold it to a printer or publisher, he could do with it as he wished. In 1616 Ben Jonson took a major step toward establishing the primacy of the play-wright by collecting and revising his plays (along with his poetry) specifically for publication and publishing them under the title *The Workes of Beniamin Jonson.* This act was taken as a sign that Jonson was putting himself and his plays on a par with classical authors and their collected works, or *Opera.* The 1640 edition added to the monumentality of the author by adding a solemn engraving of Jonson. Nonetheless, acting companies, actors, and printers still retained a great deal of control over many works. In 1633 Thomas Heywood, obviously referring to Jonson's text, wrote in his *English Traveller:* "True it is, that my playes are not exposed unto the world in Volumes, to beare the title of Workes . . . one reason is, That many of them by shifting and change of companies, have been negligently lost, Others of them are still retained in the hands of some Actors, who thinke it against their peculiar profit to have them come in Print." And although Beaumont and Fletcher were also accorded a handsome folio for their works, the fact that they collaborated on their plays undermines the later Romantic notion of the solitary genius-author. Although we tend to think of the seventeenth century as the age of Shakespeare, Lope de Vega, and Molière, one must remember that these writers only became "Authors"—in the fullest modern sense of the word—long after their deaths.

In France Pierre Corneille provides a remarkable example of how authors had to strive to define authorship. As noted, some of his plays were printed anonymously, but Corneille, like most authors, also had to face the problem of poor or pirated editions. A striking example of such dismaying errors is found in the 1665 edition of the *Tragedies et comédies* of Thomas Corneille, Pierre's brother. The engraved title page of this work, probably printed in Amsterdam "suivant la copie imprimée à Paris," contains an error that both distorts the title and alters the genre: *La Mort de l'Empereur Commode, tragédie* was transformed into *La Mort de l'Empereur, Commedie Tragedie.* Typographic errors and inconsistencies also

VERA EFFIGIES DOCTISSIMI POETARVM ANGLORVM BEN: IOHNSONII.

Ro:Vaughan fecit.

Johnsoni typus, ecce! qui furoris, | Defuncta Pater, Eruditionis,
Antistes sacer, Enthei, Camenis, | Et Scenæ veteris novator audax.
Vindex Ingenij recens Sepulti', | Nec fœlix minus, aut minus politus
Antiquæ reparator vnus artis, | Cui solus similis, Figura, Vivet.
O could there be an art found out that might
Produce his shape soe lively as to Write. Ab:Holl:

Ben Jonson, *The Workes* (1640)

wreaked havoc as printers slowly adapted to the standardization of spelling that was taking place during this period. Pierre Corneille even included an essay on spelling in his collected works to warn the reader about these changes (such as the separation of "i" and "j," "u" and "v"; accentuation conventions were also evolving). Despite the author's care, printers continued to take liberties and introduce mistakes. Taking a step toward defining the modern notion of authorship, Pierre Corneille worked closely with his editor to supervise the production of his collected works (1660). In addition to the essay on spelling mentioned above, he wrote separate and lengthy theoretical discourses on the art of writing plays for each of the first three volumes. Nor did his desire to control readings of his plays stop there. In order to answer his critics and reshape attitudes toward his corpus, he included a separate critical preface (or, rather, a self-apology), called "Examen," for each play.

Mocking Corneille's pretensions, Molière in the preface to his *Précieuses ridicules* stressed that the play was "imprimée malgré lui" ("printed in spite of him") for the sole purpose of forestalling a pirated version about to be released. Molière took the opportunity here to ridicule self-proclaimed "authors" like Corneille who appended learned discourses to their plays, proving that playwrights in search of literary glory could easily find their ambitions satirized before a skeptical public. –J.P.

Editions & Transformations: Il Pastor Fido

Print, especially in contrast to performance, is generally seen as a guarantee of a stable and regular text. However, attention to the practices of printing and the materiality of the book often reveals remarkable differences and irregularities. The practice of "stop-press correction," for example, meant that changes could be made to a text after printing had commenced. When errors were discovered or textual changes needed, only what remained of the print run would be corrected; whatever had already been printed was left unchanged. Also, different compositors setting the same text could have different preferences. The 1623 folio edition of Shakespeare's plays displays an amazing diversity among copies. Moreover, some authors (or their printers) appended different dedications to individual copies of the same edition in order to appeal to a number of different patrons.

Material differences are most vividly thrown into relief when one considers a number of editions of a single text. A fascinating example is provided by the Italian editions of Giovanni Battista Guarini's extraordinarily popular pastoral, *Il Pastor fido*. Two versions printed in 1590—one in Venice (considered the first edi-

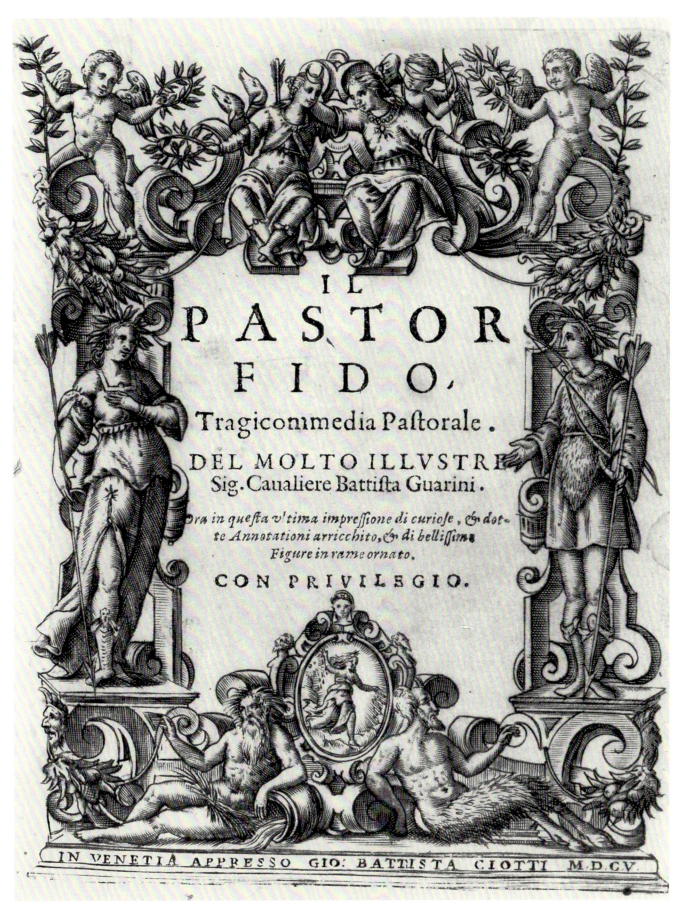

Battista Guarini, *Il Pastor fido,* (1605)

tion) and one in Ferrara—present many key variations. The Venetian edition is a quarto with a fair amount of leading, or space, between lines; it also contains a handsome printer's emblem on the title page. The one printed in Ferrara, on the other hand, is a small octavo, printed tightly without any white space and small margins, lacking illustrations and any other visual material. Printed in different parts of Italy, each carries its own privilege: the former is printed "con privilegi," while the latter announces that it is "con licenza de' Superiori." As a result of the vast popularity of the play, printers in the years following began to adorn the work with additional paratextual materials, culminating in the beautiful edition of 1602 from Venice, which renamed the author as "il molto illustre sig. cavaliere Batusta [*sic*] Guarini." This text, in an even larger format, also added an engraved portrait of the author, annotations, illustrations throughout the text, and a treatise by Guarini addressing a controversy regarding the work. The experience of reading this edition would certainly have been far different than that of reading earlier ones. Not only is the text displayed in a different style but it is supplemented with a host of other information and images. These images, furthermore, are part of a developing iconography of *Il Pastor fido*. The illustrations from earlier editions present a number of the characters in typical pastoral garb, but later editions, such as an octavo from 1659, show the characters in more formal neoclassical dress. Such transformations generate alternate meanings and emphasize different thematic aspects. In early modern books, differences in typography, page layout, format, and illustration all contribute to produce varied reading experiences. –J.P.

Crossing Borders: Translations & Adaptations

The international success of *Il Pastor fido* illustrates the power of printed drama to overcome geographical frontiers and language barriers. As early as the fifteenth century, textual exchange was facilitated by numerous book fairs at which printers from all over Europe gathered and made plays available in their original languages. In the late Renaissance, vernacular translations became common, and popular works like Guarini's pastoral circulated throughout Europe in a multitude of tongues. But at the same time that dramatic texts gained international renown, they also became subject to radical transformations. Their circulation—and recycling—was part of a larger development in which plays would swiftly shift forms as they moved not only from country to country, but from author to translator to adapter and reviser.

The Italian text of *Il Pastor fido* was printed for the first time on French soil in Tours in 1592, barely two years after its first publication in Italy, and it was almost as quickly translated into French (1593). The Guarini play was printed innumerable times during the seventeenth century, in French, Spanish, and English—and sometimes in bilingual editions. The 1676 Paris edition of *Il Pastor fido*, in Italian and French, provides a stunning example of the dual purpose of such texts. It offers itself as a pedagogical tool for learning Italian while at the same time immodestly vaunting the powers of French: according to the translator, a comparison of the two linguistic versions proves that French has words "aussi propres que les Italiens pour faire parler une passion qui nous est plus commune" ("as suitable as Italian to express an emotion more common to us"). The printed bilingual play becomes less a dramatic experience than a comparative study in modern languages.

AMARILLIS, PASTORALE.

François Passerat, *Amarillis, petite pastoralle* (1695)

Furthermore, these translations differ from the earlier humanist translations of ancient plays: for Guarini's translators the original text was a model to be loosely imitated or even surpassed in its new form. Translators regularly took great liberties, adding characters or scenes in order to adapt a play to a new culture—or simply to the adapter's own tastes. Elkanah Settle, in a 1677 English edition, did just that. Settle was self-consciously unfaithful in this version, which was in fact not based on the Italian original but rather on an earlier English translation. Richard Fanshawe's translation provides another example of how the original Italian text could become a vehicle for the translator to express his own poetic voice: he integrated *Il Pastor fido* into his own personal corpus by placing it within a volume of his own compositions.

In this context the translation could be seen—even by contemporary readers—as having lost sight of the original text. For those scrupulous readers in search of the real thing, Elzevier, the famous family of printers from Leyden and Amsterdam, produced in the second half of the seventeenth century quality pocket editions of *Il Pastor fido* in Italian, proving again that this pastoral drama had long attained the status of a canonical text in Europe.

Il Pastor fido is only one example of the textual transformations that arose from the pastoral craze in seventeenth-century Europe. While its sources can be traced back to Theocritus and Virgil, the pastoral genre was revived by sixteenth-century Italian and Spanish romances that deeply influenced later dramas. One of these founding texts is Sannazaro's *Arcadia*. Though it is a prose romance rather than a play, *Arcadia* includes passages of dialogue richly suggestive of dramatic exchange. Once writers like Guarini seized on the dramatic potential of the pastoral, its trademark elements were exploited in almost every theatrical genre, in "pastoral, pastoral-comical, historical-pastoral . . . tragical-comical-historical-pastoral," to name just a few of the dramatic categories cataloged by *Hamlet*'s belaboring Polonius. Shakespeare himself left us the most enduring and inventive play of the "pastoral-comical" tradition, *As You Like It*. And in France pastorals attained such popularity that they were even created in local dialects. Millet's *Pastorale et tragi-comédie de Janin*, for example, transforms pastoral phrasing into Grenoble's rustic patois.

The highly conventional nature of pastoral themes is conspicuous not only in the plays' language but also in the images that illustrated the editions. These engravings combine idealized nature and elegant artifice in stunning emblems of the pastoral's fusion of the rustic and the aristocratic. The frontispiece for Passerat's *Amarillis*, for example, depicts a shepherd in a Vergilian *locus amoenus*, the "pleasant place" that fuses unadorned countryside and easy comfort. At the same time, the drape hanging above the shepherd reveals the highly theatricalized nature of the setting. This artless artfulness is emblematic of a period in which aristocrats amused themselves by taking on the roles of shepherds in polite conversations and salons—as well as by literally dressing up as shepherds for portrait painters. It is no surprise that *Amarillis* was "composée pour être représentée par des personnes de qualité" ("composed to be acted by persons of quality").

However, like any well-established norm, pastoral conventions were soon lampooned in other plays. *Le Berger extravagant*, a parody of pastoral drama by Thomas Corneille (1654), is just such a play: it unmasks the absurdity of pastoral ideals by presenting a young Parisian attempting to recreate a pastoral paradise in the very real—and very unpoetic—countryside of contemporary France. He is a Don Quixote driven mad by reading not chivalric novels but many pastoral plays and romances. Yet such parodies and satires continued to co-exist with an undying love of pastoral ideals, ideals that would later inform Marie-Antoinette's hamlet at Versailles and the resurgence of nature poetry in the Romantic age.

Pastoral dramas are hardly the only example of plays handled by so many editors, translators, and adapters as to have become polymorphous. In that regard the case of Shakespeare is especially remarkable. Early folio editions of Shakespeare's works, created after the author's death, pull together plays from imperfect and varying quarto editions published in the playwright's lifetime. By the eighteenth century, Shakespeare had attained the position of a modern classical author, the most prestigious in his language, and his plays were seen not simply as dramas to be staged but as sources of moral wisdom. The 1757 edition of *Beauties of Shakespeare* testifies to the classical status that the Bard had achieved in England. Rather than conceiving of Shakespeare as a playwright, this volume presents quotations from the plays cross-referenced to ancient and modern philoso-

THE

WORKS

OF

SHAKESPEAR.

IN

SIX VOLUMES.

COLLATED and CORRECTED by the former EDITIONS,

By Mr. POPE.

  —— *Laniatum corpore toto*
Deiphobum vidi, & lacerum crudeliter ora,
Ora, manusque ambas, populataque tempora raptis
Auribus, & truncas inhonesto vulnere nares!
Quis tam crudeles optavit sumere pœnas?
Cui tantum de te licuit? ——   Virg.

LONDON:

Printed for JACOB TONSON in the *Strand.*

M DCC XXV.

William Shakespeare, *The Works* (1725)

phers and poets. Despite these radical alterations, the editor nevertheless privileged the idea of a faithful authorial text, stressing the need to establish a "correct" edition of Shakespeare's works: "The business of an editor seems to be a close attention to the text, and a careful emendation of those errors; but he should not presume to alter (and to place his alterations in the text for his author's) any passages that are not flat non-sense and contradiction." A stunning example of the attention lavished on the text and presentation of the playwright is Pope's luxurious edition of *Shakespeare's Works*. But bardolotry existed simultaneously with a trend toward "Shakespeare improvement." Works such as Nahum Tate's 1681 *History of King Lear* offer themselves as revisions and corrections of the originals, in this case providing a happy ending to the tragedy with the marriage of Edgar and Cordelia and the triumph of Lear.

Although Shakespeare epitomized the playwright *par excellence* in his own country, he was largely unknown across the channel. Indeed, the exchange between England and France had generally flowed in the other direction, as witnessed by the numerous English translations of Molière—and his marked influence on playwrights such as Wycherley, whose *Plain-dealer* (1678) was inspired by *Le Misanthrope*. However, by the 1730s Voltaire, who was exiled in England, had discovered the deep power of Shakespeare and revealed it to the French in his

Lettres écrites de Londres, where he exclaimed, "Les monstres brillants de Shakespear [sic] plaisent mille fois plus que la sagesse moderne" ("The brillant monsters of Shakespeare please infinitely more than modern wisdom"). Voltaire's praise for Shakespeare was nevertheless mixed with a strong dose of French condescension, and he was hardly a faithful translator. Indeed, he railed against the "faiseurs de traductions littérales" ("producers of literal translations") in his *Lettres*, and his own translation/adaptation of Hamlet's "To be or not to be" soliloquy is hardly recognizable to the Shakespeare connoisseur. –V.S.

Crossing Genres: Popular Theater, Parody & Critique

In France Corneille and Molière raised comedy to an elevated status, and their plays received lavish editorial attention as works of literature. However, there also existed more popular and less literary forms of comic theater, such as *parades,* farces, parodies, and *commedia dell'arte*, all of which flourished at various times from the late seventeenth through the eighteenth centuries. These comic genres, while perfectly adapted to performance at public fairs and playhouses, faced two problems inherent to their forms when transformed into print: their improvisational nature and their reliance on audience participation. Indeed, in the preface to *Théâtre italien* (a collection of works inspired by *commedia dell'arte*), the editor warned readers that the impromptu nature of the plays makes it impossible to print them faithfully: "On ne doit pas s'attendre à trouver dans ce Livre des Comédies entières, puisque les Pièces Italiennes ne sçauraient s'imprimer. La raison en est, que les Comédiens Italiens n'apprennent rien par coeur, et qu'il leur suffit, pour jouer une Comédie, d'en avoir vu le sujet un moment avant d'aller sur le Théâtre" ("One should not expect to find in this book whole Comedies, since Italian plays cannot be printed. The reason for this is that the Italian Actors learn nothing by heart; instead, in order to act a Comedy they need only to become aquainted with the subject matter just before entering the stage").

The audience participation typical of the theater performed at public fairs presents another set of problems. Spectators would regularly sing well-known tunes along with the actors or read aloud the *écriteaux* (panels) displayed above the stage. Unfortunately, this highly interactive facet of popular theater was lost on the printing press, and the only reminder of audience involvement in the theatrical production is found in the inclusion of the musical scores at the end of the volume.

Though these comic genres were quite popular, it would be wrong to assume that "low" theater and "high" culture inhabited two entirely distinct worlds. The *théâtre de la foire* and *comédie italienne* enjoyed the support of the nobility and the court, and aristocrats would in private gatherings act roles inspired by productions at fairs. More interestingly, these forms showed a surprising degree of literary self-consciousness; the authors were acutely aware of the various quarrels current in the contemporary world of letters and high theater. These popular productions were often plays about plays, explorations in the cultural battles between various theatrical genres and critical positions.

This theatrical self-consciousness was not new, as readers of Hamlet's critique of the traveling players reveals. Molière went even further in 1663, creating a play, *La Critique de l'Ecole des femmes*, that is set in a cultivated salon and that portrays—and roundly mocks—the critics of his *L'Ecole des femmes*. This type of "theater about theater" was an effective critical tool for writers of later popular drama. The Italian troupe based in France was particularly aware of the critical power of

Théâtre des boulevards, ou Recueil de parades (1756)

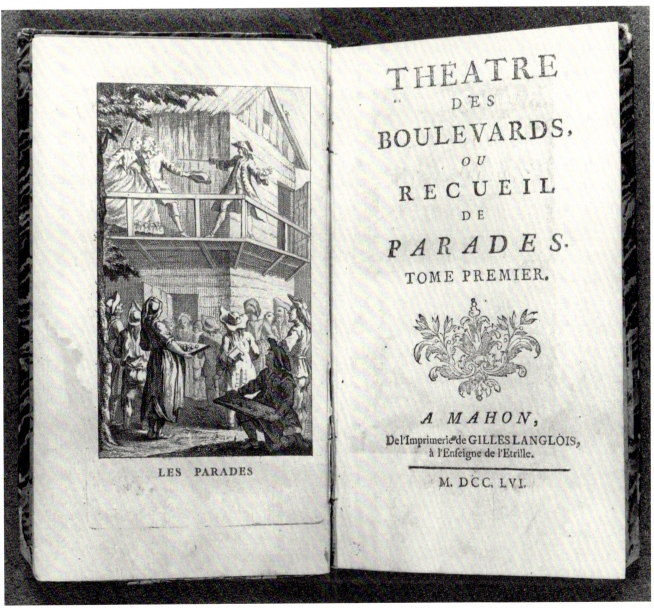

LES PARADES

THÉATRE
DES
BOULEVARDS,
OU
RECUEIL
DE
PARADES.
TOME PREMIER.

A MAHON,
De l'Imprimerie de GILLES LANGLOIS,
à l'Enseigne de l'Etrille.

M. DCC. LVI.

parodies. The editor of *Parodies du nouveau théâtre italien* did not hesitate to brag that "la parodie devient entre les mains d'un critique le flambeau dont on éclaire les défauts d'un auteur qui avait surpris l'admiration" ("parody in the hands of a critic becomes the torch with which one sheds light on the weaknesses of an author who had provoked temporary admiration"). Nothing was safe from the satirical parodies of the *Italiens,* neither the tragedies of Voltaire nor the royal operas of Quinault and Lully. Likewise, the popular *théâtre de la foire* took on the major critical debates of the day, mocking the Quarrel of the Ancients and the Moderns that raged among leading intellectuals and staging a *Querelle des Théâtres* in which each individual troupe (the *Comédie Française* and *Comédie Italienne,* the *Foire* and the Opera) battled for dominance in the turbulent Parisian theater scene. –V.S.

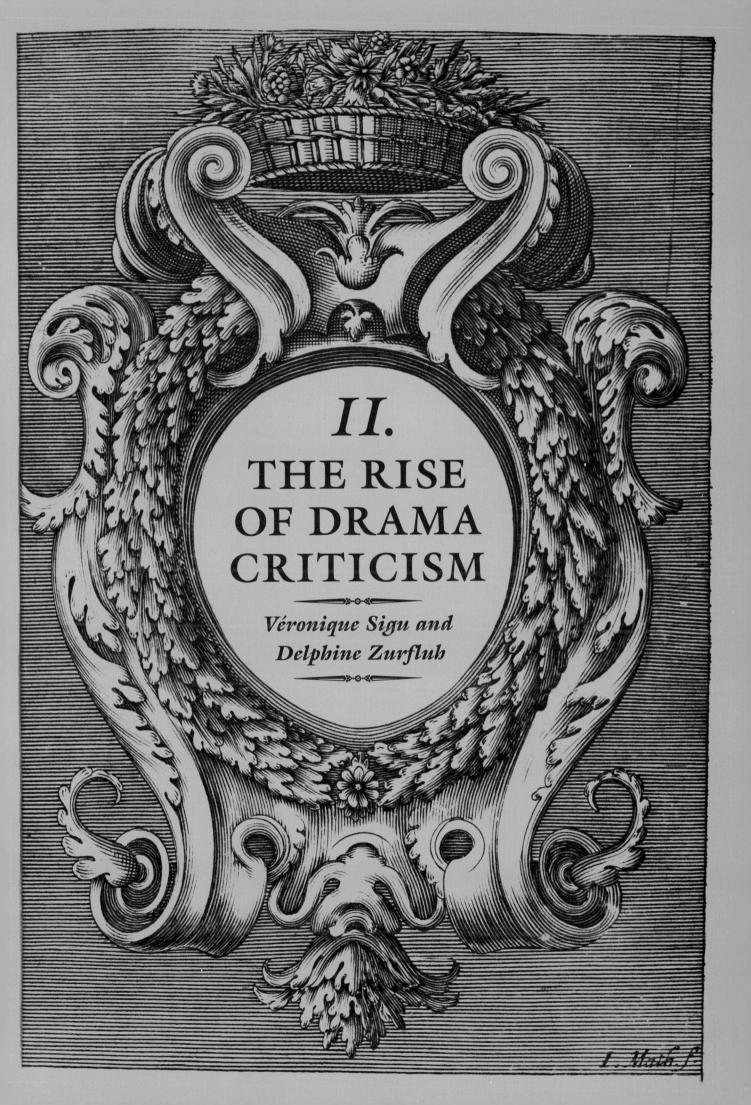

II.
THE RISE
OF DRAMA
CRITICISM

Véronique Sigu and
Delphine Zurfluh

THE RISE OF DRAMA CRITICISM

Theoretical Treatises & Critical Essays

Just as Renaissance humanists devoted themselves to editing and glossing ancient plays, so too did they bring their attention to bear on the theoretical aspects of theater. Sixteenth- and early seventeenth-century scholars worked principally from two ancient treatises on dramatic poetry, Aristotle's *Poetics* and Horace's *Art of Poetry*. These Renaissance commentaries were devoted primarily to understanding ancient drama rather than to guiding modern playwrights. Nevertheless, from their devotion to antiquity was born a new and highly modern theory of theater that transformed dramatic criticism.

The primacy of the ancient texts in these humanist reflections on drama is graphically illustrated in a bilingual 1643 edition of the Dutch scholar Heinsius's *De Tragoediæ constitutione liber*, in which the author appended Aristotle's original text, in both Greek and Latin, to his own neo-Latin commentary. Here, Heinsius followed the tradition of the late Italian Renaissance in not only reviving but, more importantly, radically reworking Aristotle's thinking on the theater. Two of the most important Italian theoreticians of drama in the mid-sixteenth century, Castelvestro and Scaliger, interpolated from the *Poetics* a series of rules for the theater (concerning the unities of time, place and action and the constraints of decorum) that molded the neoclassical style of drama that later dominated in France and Restoration England. The page layout of a 1570 edition of *La Poetica d'Aristotele* offers an excellent visual example of this method of liberal exegesis: Castelvestro offered first a brief passage of the Greek text, followed by a brief description (*contenenza*), a translation (*vulgarizzamento*), and finally a commentary (*spositi-*

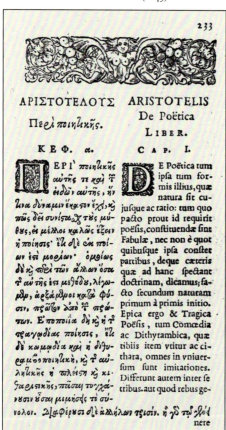

Daniel Heinsius, *De tragoediæ constitutione liber* (1643)

Nicolas Boileau Despréaux, *Oeuvres* (1718)

one). Scaliger gave himself even more theoretical license in his own reflection on theater, the 1561 *Poetices libri septem*, offering perhaps the most influential—and original—neo-Aristotelian theory of drama.

All of this theorizing had a striking impact on practice. As theater reached new heights of cultural prestige in the seventeenth century, the *Poetics* became a subject of debate not only among theoreticians and learned playwrights but also among a broader public passionate about theater and its rules. André Dacier's French translation and elegant commentary in *La Poétique* is indicative of this wider interest. However, well before Dacier other writers had taken a pragmatic layman's approach to dramatic theory, as is demonstrated by the very title of the Abbé d'Aubignac's influential *La Pratique du théâtre* (1657). This book presents itself on the title page as a work intended not for intellectuals but rather for practicing playwrights and interested theatergoers, for "tous ceux qui veulent s'appliquer à la composition des poemes dramatiques...ou qui prennent plaisir d'en voir les représentations." ("all who wish to apply themselves to writing dramatic poems ...or who take pleasure in seeing them represented"). The vogue for theory had flowered not only in the playhouses of Paris but also in the salons of high society.

Playwrights of course did not hesitate to join in debates over the "rules of art." While some dramatists, such as Corneille, chose to write theoretical prefaces to their works, others wrote and published independent treatises on theater. John Dryden's *Of Dramatick Poesie* and Lope de Vega's *El Nuevo Arte de hazer comedias en este tiempo,* a critical work in verse first read to a learned academy, are only two of the most prominent.

In addition to the work of scholars and playwrights, theater criticism became a general subject of *belles lettres* and conversational exchange. Reflections on the theater, in prose and poetry, were written in an easy non-academic style to a general, if elite, public. The case of Boileau's 1674 *Art poétique* is emblematic here. A work in elegant verse, the poem was first read by its author before publication in the non-scholarly setting of a Parisian salon. In a style more polished than learned, *L'Art poétique* reflects on ancient and modern playwrights, on the heroes of tragedy and the scandals of farce, on dramatic rules and audience taste. Despite this unpedantic approach, the erudition of the author—and his theoretical authority—were later enhanced in printed versions of the work, first with his own annotations and then with additional commentaries in a 1718 edition, published less than a decade after his death. The title page of this edition visually elevates Boileau to the learned humanist tradition with a portrait of him held aloft above Apollo, the Muses, and editions of ancient Greek and Latin authors. By contrast, another critic of the time, Saint-Evremond, maintained in print a less daunting and more intimate aspect, with editions reminding the reader that his own "dissertations" on Racine originated in the social exchange of letter writing. In both cases, though, it is clear that reflections on theater had entered the heart of both social and literary life; the stage was set for the birth of journalistic drama criticism. –D.Z.

Letters & Periodicals

One of the most significant developments in the world of seventeenth-century letters is undoubtedly the birth of the periodical. In France by the mid-seventeenth century, nascent periodical forms such as Loret's *Muse historique* routinely printed brief accounts of the Paris stage in its doggerel verse review of court and town life. However, it was Donneau de Visé's *Mercure galant,* created in 1672, that most closely approached what we think of today as journalism by publishing chatty, in-depth prose descriptions of contemporary literary and social life—including lively and provocative pieces on the theater. In doing so, *Le Mercure galant* greatly expanded the arena for debates in contemporary drama, opening the theater scene up to a much wider cultivated public, particularly women, in the provinces far beyond Paris. In England the most brilliant example was *The Spectator*, begun by Joseph Addison and Richard Steele in 1711. In these elegant and witty pages, the theater fascinates not only as a place to view new plays but perhaps even more importantly as a site for the journalist's keen social observation into the fashions and fads of the elite London theater-going public.

Innovative as such periodicals as *Le Mercure galant* and *The Spectator* were, their treatment of theater has important literary antecedents. These new journals were, after all, commercialized and popularized versions of a much older tradition: letter writing. The great French letter writer of the seventeenth century, Madame de Sévigné, offers some striking examples of the critical tone and attitudes adopted by private correspondents in their theater commentary. For instance, when sending Racine's *Bajazet* to her daughter in distant Provence, she stressed the splendors of an actress's performance, which could never be captured in print: "If I could send you Champmêlée [i.e. Champmeslé] at the same time, you would find more beauties in it, for without the actress the piece loses half its merit." This passage perfectly demonstrates the tastes of a cultivated non-professional spectator of the time, tastes that could easily value a good performance above a good read. Despite the seemingly intimate nature of personal correspondence, some literary figures (such as Saint-Evremond) published their letters during their lifetime; Madame de Sévigné's correspondence, however, was first published in 1725, nearly thirty years after her death.

As the eighteenth century progressed, more specialized periodicals arose that focused on the theater. A new kind of publication, theater almanacs, cataloged in great detail contemporary theatrical representations, carefully listing actors, authors, theaters, dancers, and musicians. One such almanac, *Les Spectacles de Paris,* was first printed in 1752 as the *Almanach historique et chronologique de tous les spectacles* and was published without interruption until 1794. The days of gleaning information about new plays from private letters were over; the press had transformed the early modern triumph of theater into a victory for itself. –V.S.

The SPECTATOR.

Qualis ubi audito venantum murmure Tigris
Horruit in maculas———Statius.

Saturday, June 2. 1711.

ABOUT the middle of laſt Winter I went to ſee an *Opera* at the Theatre in the *Hay-Market*, where I could not but take notice of two Parties of very Fine Women, that had placed themſelves in the oppoſite Side-Boxes, and ſeemed drawn up in a kind of Battel Array one againſt another. After a ſhort Survey of them, I found they were *Patched* differently; their Faces, on one Hand, being Spotted on the Right Side of the Forehead, and that upon the other on the Left. I quickly perceived that they caſt Hoſtile Glances upon one another; and that their Patches were placed in thoſe different Situations, as Party Signals to diſtinguiſh Friends from Foes. In the Middle-Boxes, between theſe two oppoſite Bodies, were ſeveral Ladies who Patched indifferently on both ſides of their Faces, and ſeemed to ſit there with no other Intention but to ſee the *Opera*. Upon Enquiry I found that the Body of *Amazons* on my Right Hand were Whigs, and thoſe on my Left, Tories; and that thoſe who had placed themſelves in the Middle-Boxes were a Neutral Party, whoſe Faces had not yet declared themſelves. Theſe laſt however, as I afterwards found, diminiſhed daily, and took their Party with one Side or the other, inſomuch that I obſerved in ſeveral of them, the Patches which were before diſperſed equally, are now all gone over to the Whig or Tory Side of the Face. The Cenſorious ſay, That the Men whoſe Hearts are aimed at are very often the Occaſions that one part of the Face is thus Diſhonoured, and lyes under a kind of Diſgrace, while the other is ſo much Set off and Adorned by the Owner; and that the Patches turn to the Right or to the Left, according to the Principles of the Man who is moſt in Favour. But whatever may be the Motives of a few Fantaſtical Coquets, who do not Patch for the Publick Good, ſo much as for their own Private Advantage, it is certain that there are ſeveral Women of Honour who Patch out of Principle, and with an Eye to the Intereſt of their Country. Nay, I am informed, that ſome of them adhere ſo ſtedfaſtly to their Party, and are ſo far from Sacrificing their Zeal for the Publick to their Paſſion for any particular Perſon, that in a late Draught of Marriage Articles a Lady has ſtipulated with her Huſband, That, whatever his Opinions are, ſhe ſhall be at Liberty to Patch on which ſide ſhe pleaſes.

I muſt here take notice, that *Roſalinda*, a Famous Whig Partizan, has moſt unfortunately a very beautiful Mole on the Tory part of her Forehead, which, being very conſpicuous, has occaſioned many Miſtakes, and given an Handle to her Enemies to miſrepreſent her Face, as though it had Revolted from the Whig Intereſt. But whatever this natural Patch may ſeem to intimate, it is well known that her Notions of Government are ſtill the ſame. This unlucky Mole however has miſ-led ſeveral Coxcombs, and, like the hanging out of falſe Colours, made ſome of them Converſe with *Roſalinda* in what they thought the Spirit of her Party, when on a ſudden ſhe has given them an unexpected Fire, that has ſunk them all at once. If *Roſalinda* is unfortunate in her Mole, *Nigranilla* is as unhappy in a Pimple which forces her, againſt her Inclinations, to Patch on the Whig ſide.

I am told that many Virtuous Matrons, who formerly have been taught to believe that this Artificial Spotting of the Face was unlawful, are now reconciled by a Zeal for their Cauſe, to what they could not be prompted by a Concern for their Beauty. This way of declaring War upon one another, puts me in mind of what is reported of the Tigreſs, that ſeveral Spots riſe in her Skin when ſhe is angry; or as Mr. *Cowley* has imitated the Verſes that ſtand as the Motto of this Paper,

———She Swells with angry Pride,
And calls forth all her Spots on every ſide.

When I was in the Theatre the time above-mentioned, I had the Curioſity to count the Patches on both Sides, and found the Tory Patches to be about twenty Stronger than the Whig; but to make amends for this ſmall Inequality, I the next Morning found the whole Puppet-ſhow filled with Faces ſpotted after the Whiggiſh manner. Whether or no the Ladies had retreated hither in order to rally their Forces I cannot tell, but the next Night they came in ſo great a Body to the Opera, that they out-numbered the Enemy.

This Account of Party-Patches will, I am afraid, appear improbable to thoſe who live at a diſtance from the faſhionable World, but as it is a Diſtinction of a very ſingular Nature, and what perhaps may
never

The Spectator (1711-1712)

Religious Criticism

Though early modern scholars, playwrights, and journalists all helped to create a new way of writing about drama, it was not just theater sympathizers who exploited the printing press. The religious enemies of theater were also busy penning their own essays and pamphlets. As the discussion of censorship has shown, the relationship between Church and theater is long and troubled. And a glance at Restoration England and the France of Louis XIV illustrates that even during the best of times for the playhouse, moral attacks proved a fertile ground for print polemics.

At the very moment that French theater reached new cultural heights under the Sun King, religious critics strengthened their condemnations of the stage. A host of anti-theatrical treatises, by such authors as Armand de Bourbon, Prince de Conti, attempted to turn public opinion against drama. The attacks of course did not go unanswered. Treatise engendered treatise, and playwrights published their defenses of the stage. The comic author Boursault, for example, adopted a keen editorial strategy in his own quarrel with religious critics; rather than defend himself with his own words, he supplemented his collected *Pièces de théâtre* with an authoritative endorsement entitled "Lettre d'un Théologien illustre par la qualité et par son mérite, consulté par l'Auteur, pour sçavoir si la Comédie peut être permise, ou doit être absolument deffendue" ("Letter of a theologian of famous worth and merit, consulted by the author to know if the comedy can be allowed or must be entirely prohibited"). Boursault had reason to seek such approval: His own play *Esope à la cour* had previously been censored for alleged impiety.

In England puritanical opposition to theater led to the closing of the playhouses under Oliver Cromwell. However, as in France, royal patronage and popular favor revived the theater during the Restoration, and religious polemicists did not hide their disgust. The most notorious example is the 1698 treatise by the Anglican clergyman Jeremy Collier, *A Short View of the Immorality and Profaneness of the English*

Jeremy Collier, *A Short View of the Immorality and Profaneness of the English Stage* (1698)

THE

PREFACE.

BEing convinc'd that nothing has gone farther in Debauching the Age than the Stage-Poets, and Play-House, I thought I could not employ my time better than in Writing against them. These Men sure, take Vertue and Regularity, for great Enemies, why else is their Disaffection so very Remarkable: It must be said, they have made their Attack with great Courage, and gain'd no inconsiderable Advantage. But it seems Lewdness without Atheism, is but half their Business. Conscience might possibly recover, and Revenge be

A 2   thought

Stage. Collier savaged English theater, and in particular comic playwrights like Congreve, for such redoubtable sins as mocking the clergy. This particular complaint turned even more personal—and theatrical—after the 1700 opening of Congreve's *The Way of the World,* in which *A Short View* is openly derided. More importantly, Congreve defended himself formally with his counter-polemic, *Amendments of Mr Collier's False and Imperfect Citations, &c.,* which in turn provoked Collier's reply, *Defence of the Short View.* Indeed, Collier made a profession of printing pamphlets against the theater, spurred on by his opponents' replies. Thus, the printing presses profited from the polemics while the playhouses flourished with profane delights. –V. S.

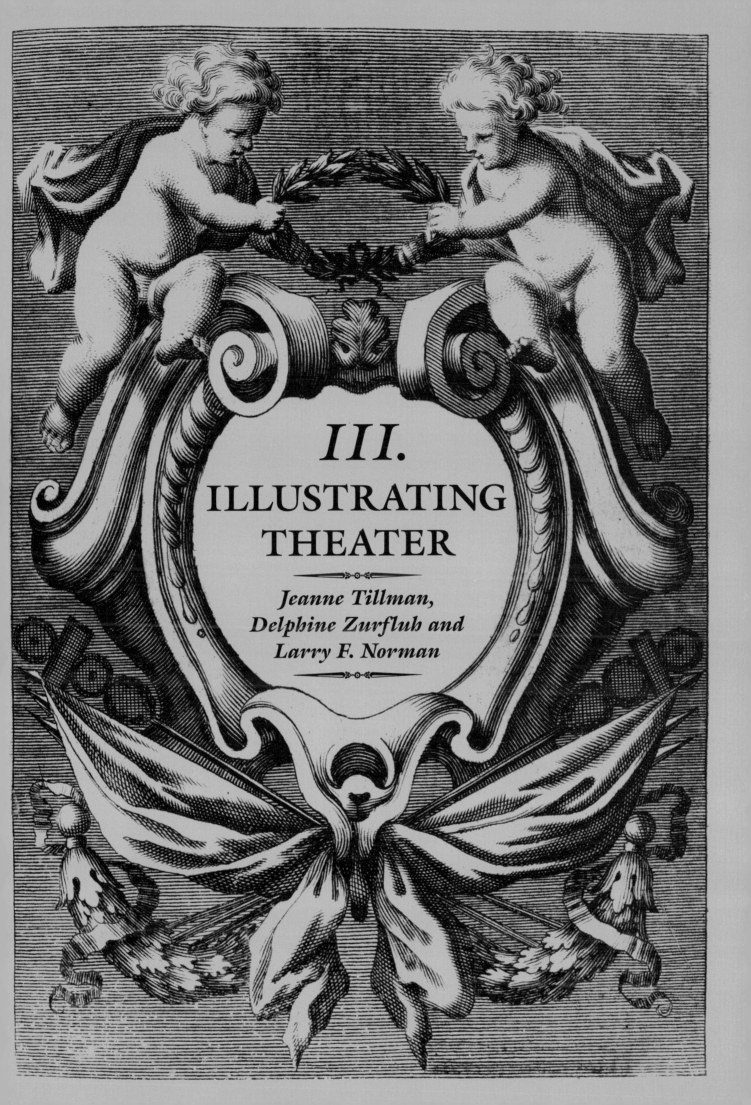

III.
ILLUSTRATING
THEATER

Jeanne Tillman,
Delphine Zurfluh and
Larry F. Norman

ILLUSTRATING THEATER

Frontispieces: Sets or Setting?

The frontispiece plays a rich and ambiguous role for readers first confronting a dramatic text. In order to seize the imagination, opening illustrations aim toward contradictory ends, endeavoring alternately to reproduce the stage set faithfully and to abandon the playhouse altogether by evoking the true setting of the story. They are images that exist in a constant tension between the actual set and an idealized setting, between an accurate representation of stage productions (flat backdrops, raised stage floor, dramatic curtains) and a transcendental evocation of the fictional space depicted in all its untheatrical details. Sometimes we see actors on stage, sometimes real people in thick woods or on a turbulent sea; sometimes we see scenes exactly as played on stage, sometimes fantastic actions never acted but only narrated by other characters.

Jean-Baptiste Molière, *Les Oeuvres* (1691)

L'IMPROMPTU DE VERSAILLES

The frontispiece for Molière's *L'Ecole des femmes* illustrates perfectly the tendency toward a faithful reproduction of stage decor. The facades of the houses are transparently flat backdrops; they meet the equally smooth stage floor (which makes no attempt to disguise itself as pavement) in a thud of two-dimensional right angles. Furthermore, the skewed perspective, with actors nearly as tall as houses, reflects all too well the representational imperfections of the comic stage. Likewise, the contrived balcony window scene depicted in *L'Etourdy ou du Contre-Temps* adheres to the scale of an entirely conventional set rather than that of a true city scene.

In other cases it is not the practical elements of set construction but instead the more emblematic signs of the theater that transport the reader

Battista Guarini, *Il Pastor fido* (1602)

to the playhouse. Frontispieces often depict the raised floor of the stage (*L'Ecole des maris; Le Misanthrope*). These images are further theatricalized by the appearance of a draping banner announcing the title of the play and suggesting the kind of publicizing activities that surrounded dramatic productions. Billowing curtains also add a theatrical element to the image, emphasized in the frontispiece to an English printing of *Le Cid* by the perfectly posed group of actors and their highly rhetorical postures. The excesses of stagey acting styles are most perfectly conveyed, however, in the frontispiece to *L'Impromptu de Versailles*, a play in which Molière portrayed himself in the act of rehearsing his new comedy with his troupe. In the scene depicted, Molière cruelly imitates before an audience of his fellow actors the grand histrionics of famous French actors, parodying their worn gestures and overwrought declamation.

This image from *L'Impromptu* shows just how far frontispieces can go in their reflection on theatrical performance. However, reflection on the nature of drama could also lead illustrators away from the reality of the stage and toward more allegorical representations. The illustrations to a 1602 Venice edition of *Il Pastor fido* stunningly reflect this tendency toward the emblematic and the fantastic. In this edition each of the five acts is illustrated with a separate landscape engraving in which every individual scene from the act is depicted as a discrete grouping in the landscape. These groupings of characters recede toward the horizon following the order of their place in the action: the foreground represents the first scene, the background the last scene. In this manner the image idealizes the perfect unity of the act structure while still presenting each of the scenes that constitutes it. The temporality of each act collapses beautifully into a single pictorial moment.

Of course the landscape represented here is hardly one that could be reproduced with such nuance on a baroque stage. But this kind of idealization is typical of the tendency toward transcendence that animates many frontispieces. The image of Hades from *L'Ombre de Molière*, with its three-headed Cerberus and its swirling background, like the swelling sea tides depicted in Corneille's *La Mort de Pompée*, are sumptuously depicted without regard to the limitations of stage decor and machinery. Indeed, this infidelity to actual stage production led some editors to choose images that were never staged at all. This is particularly true of editions produced in France, where the rules of decorum prohibited scenes of physical violence on stage. Frontispieces, consequently, often present bloody struggles that audiences never viewed but instead learned about from entering messengers (*Horace; Sertorius*). Yet even in these unstaged scenes, the theatrical exuberance of the tragic actor recalls the playhouse, never entirely absent from the baroque imagination. –D.Z./L.N.

Perspective & Italian Set Design

The triumph of the theater was expressed not only in dramatic masterpieces and new forms of criticism; it also shone through in new architectural design for the stage. Baroque stage design began with an explosion of interest in the classical architect Vitruvius and his *De Architectura*. This revival was part of the humanist focus on classical texts. *De Architectura* was first printed in 1487; by the end of the sixteenth century, there had been over twenty-five editions. Among the most influential was the 1521 edition, with commentary by humanist painter-architect Cesare Cesariano and with illustrations that show Renaissance and baroque architects how to integrate Vitruvian precepts into their own work.

Vitruvius described sets made up of *periaktoi*, or prisms, "which revolve, each having three decorated faces." The set walls were painted with scenes in perspec-

Vitruvius Pollio, *Les Dix Livres d'architecture de Vitruve* (1684)

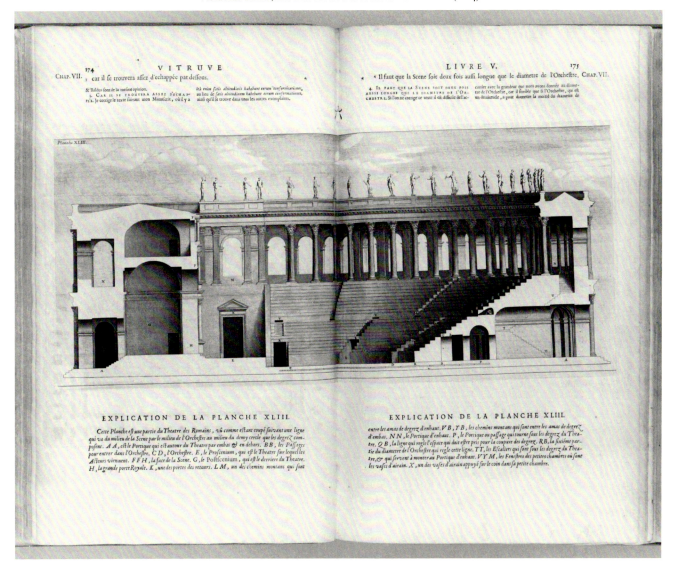

tive to a false horizon, "so that by this deception a faithful representation of the appearance of buildings might be given in painted scenery." Vitruvius' work led to two divergent theories. Jacomo Barozzi da Vignola recreated Vitruvius' *periaktoi*, but his work was overshadowed by that of the influential architect Sebastian Serlio. Serlio's *Architettura* went through many editions and was translated into French and German. Serlio originally intended his *Architettura* to simply extend Vitruvius' work; that he ended by becoming a revered master of architecture and set design perfectly illustrates the Renaissance aim of emulating and transcending the ancients. Though Serlio chose to build flat sets instead of *periaktoi*, he benefited from—and improved upon—Vitruvian perspective theory. His innovation was to move the horizon to beyond the back of the theater, thereby improving the set's realism. This vanishing point became the focus for both stage and set construction. The stage was inclined at the back, with a series of grooves cut into its floor. Canvas flats, painted with geometrically precise designs, were propped up in the floor-grooves. The next major innovator in set design, Roman painter and set-designer Andrea Pozzo, improved upon the Serlian model. He refined perspectival mathematics, producing flats that revealed ornate, labyrinthine buildings; he then detailed his method in *Prospettiva de' pittori e architetti*, permitting other architects to create innumerable sets of apparently endless Vitruvian-style cityscapes.

Like Vitruvius and Serlio, whose discussions of theater construction appeared in books on architecture, Pozzo presented his ideas on set design in a book on a broader topic, in his case perspective painting. However, the interest in theater as such was growing as courts, academies and public theaters developed more complex forms of stage machinery and design. By the mid-seventeenth century, more practical, stage-oriented works such as *Le Mémoire de Mahelot* (1673), one of the first books exclusively devoted to set design, began to appear. Freed from its dependence on its sister arts, the stage space had finally taken its place as an autonomous subject for authors, printers, and engravers. –J.T.

The Baroque Pageant

Court set designers joined with costume designers, choreographers, musicians, poets, and landscape architects to create spectacular baroque festivals. These court pageants were dramatic productions, performed outside of the typical theatrical space and on a grander scale than an ordinary theater could offer. Pageant forms varied greatly, but their sources and aims were identical. Baroque festivals grew out of classical pageants, and they often alluded to ancient history and mythology. The pageant's purpose was always the same: to dazzle its audience. Stage machinery created visual wonder. A splendid example is provided by the climactic scene of *La Sincerita trionfante*, a production staged in Rome in 1640, where the goddess

Ottaviano Castelli, *La Sincerita trionfante, overo l' Erculeo ardire* (1640)

Minerva appeared floating on a cloud. This effect was achieved by attaching a painted flat to a movable beam controlled by pulleys. The performer stood on the platform, and the goddess appeared on a cloud. At other pageants, fireworks shot out of silk flats, or sea serpents moved through water.

Courtiers themselves took roles in the pageants; their participation indicates the festivals' real import. Magnificent pageants reassured their audiences of the monarch's splendor and reinforced the image of power. To further this end, the pageants were memorialized in fete books, becoming powerful political tools. Eight years after its staging, *Festiva ad capita . . . ,* was published by the royal press in neo-Latin, complete with spectacular engravings; it effectively served as a sign of Louis XIV's magnificence during a propaganda war between the French king and the Hapsburgs. The pageant itself was an ephemeral event; the fete book offered lasting proof of the monarch's power.

The most familiar pageant form is the English masque, a private spectacle frequently staged at Whitehall Palace for the exclusive pleasure of the Stuart courts of James I and Charles I (1605–40). Staging—engineered by Inigo Jones— was crucial to the masque's success. Jones, the architect for the Stuart court, designed the banquet hall at Whitehall Palace and engineered the Stuart masques.

Detail from
Charles Perrault, *Festiva ad capita annulumque decursio* (1670)

He created moving or revolving stages, flying chariots, and floating islands populated with gods and fire spirits. On Jones's sets, loosely plotted political allegories—most frequently and famously by Ben Jonson—were depicted in verse and dance. The first part of the performance was devoted to the antimasque, in which actors in grotesque costumes performed outlandish dances. Eventually, these dancers were banished and replaced by the masquers—courtiers dressed as gods or heroes, silently illustrating the masque's theme in choreographed dances.

Masque audiences and performers were more interested in the spectacle than the allegory; masque authors changed over time, but Inigo Jones was indispensable. But a masque, like any pageant or play, was an ephemeral event. Masques were not preserved in fete-book form, although masque-texts were published. In the 1616 edition of his *Works*, Jonson included all of his previously performed masques and gave a sense of the masque and the problems he experienced working with Jones. The introduction to one of the masques reveals his agenda—to establish the poetic text as the single most important feature of the collaborative production. Comparing the spectacle of the masque to the body and its text to the soul, he wrote: "So short-lived are the bodies of all things, in comparison of their souls. And though bodies oft-times have the ill luck to be sensually preferred, they find afterwards, the good fortune (when souls live) to be utterly forgotten." To insure the lasting impression of his contribution, Jonson abbreviated, eliminated, and even took credit for aspects of the staging. For example, Jones created some wonderful sets for the 1611 masque *Love Freed from Ignorance and Folly*, including a cloud-borne arrival for the masquers. But in his publication of the masque-text, Jonson included no description of this scene; in fact, he included no descriptions of either sets or costumes for the entire masque.

In happy contrast to Jonson (at least in terms of our understanding of these splendid productions), William Davenant gave full descriptions of Jones's staging for their collaborations. But description alone cannot convey the full visual experience of a masque, and unfortunately the published masque-texts were never illustrated with Jones's sketches. Jones's masque designs were eventually sold and dispersed; they were not published until long after his death. The unfinished quality of Jones's surviving sketches ultimately proves the mutual dependence of pageant and book. While the visual wonder depicted in fete books may be a mere shadow of the glory that was, they were the only means of preserving an ephemeral art form. The baroque spectacle may be lost forever, but its specter is still evoked in print. –J.T.

CHECKLIST

PROLOGUE
HUMANISM

Plautus (250–184 B.C.E.). *Plautus integer cum interpretatione.* Milan: Uldericus Scinzenzeler, 1500.

Plautus. *Sarssinatis Comedie XX.* [Lyon: B. de Gabiano for B. Trot, 1513].

Plautus. *Ex Plauti Comoediis.* Venice: In aedibus Aldi, and Andreae Asulani, 1522.

Plautus. *Comoedia XX.* Neustadt an der Weinstrasse: Haeredes Jacobus Fischer, 1619. Berlin Collection

Seneca (ca. 4 B.C.E.–65 C.E.). *Seneca: His Tenne Tragedies.* London: Thomas Marsh, 1581.

Sophocles (ca. 496–406 B.C.E.). *Sophoclis tragaediae septem cum commentariis.* Venice: Aldus Manutius, 1502. The Helen and Ruth Regenstein Collection of Rare Books

Sophocles. *Edipo tiranno, tragedia di Sofocle.* Florence: Bartolomeo Sermartelli, 1589. Gift of Howard Weingrow

Terence (ca. 19–159 B.C.E.). *P Terentii aphri comico [rum] elegantissimi comedie.* [Lyon?]: Stephen Balan, 1505.

Terence. *Las Seys Comedias de Terentio.* Alcala: Juan Gracian, 1583.

I.
PLAYS, PRINTING AND PUBLICS

Performance & Printing

Francis Beaumont (1584–1616) and John Fletcher (1579–1625). *Philaster or, Love Lies a Bleeding.* 6th impression. London: Printed for William Leake, [1661?].

George Chapman (1559?–1634). *The Revenge of Bussy D'Ambois., A Tragedie.* London: T.S., 1613.

De Chapoton (fl. 1638–1648). *Le veritable Coriolan, Tragedie.* Paris: Toussainct Quinet, 1638. The Helen and Ruth Regenstein Collection of Rare Books

Heliodorus (fl. ca. 220). *Les chastes, et loyales amours de Theagene et Cariclée.* Adapt. by Alexandre Hardy. 2nd ed., rev. and corr. Paris: Jacques Quesnel, 1628.

Ben Jonson (1573?–1637). *The Divell is an Asse.* London: n.p., 1641. Celia and Delia Austrian Study Collection

Pierre de Larivey (ca. 1540–1619). *Les Comedies facecieuses à l'imitation des anciens Grecs, Latins, & modernes Italiens.* 2nd ed. Lyon: Benoist Rigaud, 1597.

John Lilly (1554?–1606). *Sixe Court Comedies.* London: Printed by William Stansby for Edward Blount, 1632.

John Marston (1575?–1634). *The Malcontent,* by Ihon Webster. London: Printed by V. S[immes] for William Aspley, 1604. Celia and Delia Austrian Study Collection

Thomas Middleton (d. 1627) and William Rowley (1585?–1642?). *A Faire Quarrell.* London: Printed for I. T., 1617.

Jean-Baptiste Molière (1622–1673). *Les Œuvres.* Rev., corr., and augm. Vol. 4. Paris: Denys Thierry, Claude Barbin, et Pierre Trabouillet, 1697.

Thomas Nabbes (1605?–1645?). *The Unfortunate Mother: A Tragedie.* London: Printed by J. O. for Daniell Frere, 1640.

M. [Georges] de Scudéry (1601–1667). *La Mort de Cæsar, tragedie.* 2nd ed. Paris: Augustin Courbé, 1637. The Helen and Ruth Regenstein Collection of Rare Books

The Power of Audiences

Francis Beaumont (1584–1616) and John Fletcher (1579–1625). *The Knight of the Burning Pestle.* London: Printed by N. O[kes] for J. S[pencer], 1635.

Daubridgcourt Belchier (1580?–1621). *Hans Beer-Pot.* London: Bernard Alsop, 1618.

Pierre Corneille (1606–1684) and Thomas Corneille (1625–1709). *Tragedie.* Trans. by Francese dal Canonico Antonio Francesco Ghiselli. 3 vols. [Bologna, ca. 1690–1700]. Manuscript copies, probably in the hand of the translator, with printed programs of dramatic performances.

Du Cercau (1670–1730). *Les Incommodités de la grandeur.* Paris: Thiboust, 1747.

Pierre Le Hayer du Perron (1603–1679?). *Les Heureuses Advantures, trage-comedie.* Paris: Anthoine de Sommaville, 1633.

Claude-François Menestrier (1631–1705). *L'Autel de Lyon.* Lyon: Jean Molin, 1658. The Helen and Ruth Regenstein Collection of Rare Books

Jean-Baptiste Molière (1622–1673). *Les Œuvres.* Rev., corr., and augm. Vol. 2. Paris: Denys Thierry, Claude Barbin, et Pierre Trabouillet, 1697.

Philippe Quinault (1635–1688). [*Les Opéras du Roy.* Paris, 1676–77].

Philippe Quinault. *Ballet de la jeunesse, divertissement.* N.p., n.d., after the 1686 Paris edition.

James Shirley (1596–1666). *The Triumph of Peace. A Masque.* London: Printed by John Norton for William Cooke, 1633.

Regulators & Censors

Giovanni Nicolò Boldoni (1595–1670). *L'Annuntiata.* Bologna: Per l'Herede del Benacci, 1636. The Helen and Ruth Regenstein Collection of Rare Books

William D'Avenant (1606–1668). *The Witts.* London: Printed for Richard Meighen, 1636.

Thomas Middleton (d. 1627). *A Game at Chess.* [London]: n.p., [1625?]. Celia and Delia Austrian Study Collection

Jean-Baptiste Molière (1622–1673). *Les Oeuvres.* New ed. Vol. 3. Amsterdam: Henri Wetstein, 1691. Gift of Julius Rosenwald

Jean-Baptiste Molière. *Les Œuvres.* Rev., corr., and augm. Vols. 5, 7. Paris: Denys Thierry, Claude Barbin, et Pierre Trabouillet, 1697.

William Prynne (1600–1669). *Histrio-mastix. The Players Scourge, or Actors Tragædie.* London: Printed by E. A. and W. I. for Michael Sparke, 1633. The Frederic Ives Carpenter Memorial Collection

M. Scarron (1610–1660). *Le Jodelet, ou le m^e valet, comedie.* Paris: Toussainct Quinet, 1645.

M. Scarron. *Le Jodelet, ou le maistre valet. Comedie.* Rouen: Antoine Ferrand, 1654. From the Bequest of Professor Bernard Weinberg

The Birth of the Playwright

Lodovico Ariosto (1474–1533). *Comedia…Cassaria.* Venice: Marchio Sessa, 1536.

L'Aveugle de Smyrne. Tragi-comédie par les cinq autheurs. Paris: Augustin Courbé, 1638. The Helen and Ruth Regenstein Collection of Rare Books

Francis Beaumont (1584–1616) and John Fletcher (1579–1625). *Fifty Comedies and Tragedies.* 2nd ed. London: J. Macock, 1679.

Pierre Corneille (1606–1684). *Le Menteur, comedie.* Vol. 2. Paris: Antoine de Sommaville et Augustin Courbé, 1644. The Helen and Ruth Regenstein Collection of Rare Books

Pierre Corneille. *Le Theatre.* Vol. 1. Paris: Guillaume de Luyne, 1664.

Pierre Corneille. *Le Theatre.* Vol. 1. Paris: Estienne Loyson, 1682.

Thomas Corneille (1625–1709). *Les Tragedies et comedies.* Rev., corr, and augm. Vol. 2. [Amsterdam?: A. Wolfgang?], after the 1665 Paris edition. Gift of Julius Rosenwald

Bernardo da Bibbiena Dovizi (1470–1520). *La Calandra.* Venice: Plinio Pietrasanta, 1554.

Ben Jonson (1573?–1637). *The Workes.* 2nd ed. London: Richard Bishop, 1640.

Thomas Middleton (d. 1627). *A Mad World, My Masters.* London: Printed for J. S., 1640.

Jean-Baptiste Molière (1622–1673). *Les Œuvres.* Rev., corr., and augm. Vol. 1. Paris: Denys Thierry, Claude Barbin, et Pierre Trabuillet, 1682. Gift of Julius Rosenwald

Swetnam, The Woman Hater, Arraigned by Women. London: Printed for Richard Meighen, 1620.

Editions & Transformations: Il Pastor Fido

Battista Guarini (1538–1612). *Il Pastor fido.* Venice: Gio. Battista Bonfadino, 1590.

Battista Guarini. *Il Pastor fido.* Ferrara: Benedetto Mamarello, 1590.

Battista Guarini. *Il Pastor fido.* Venice: Gio. Battista Ciotti, 1602. From the Bequest of Professor Bernard Weinberg

Battista Guarini. *Il Pastor fido.* Venice: Gio. Battista Ciotti, 1605. Purchased from a fund given in honor of Herman H. Fussler by Bernard Weinberg

Battista Guarini. *Il Pastor fido.* Venice: Gio. Battista Ciotti, 1621.

Crossing Borders: Translations & Adaptations

Thomas Corneille (1625–1709). *Le Berger extravagant; pastorale burlesque.* Rouen: Laurens Maurry, 1654.

Battista Guarini (1538–1612). *Il Pastor fido.* Amsterdam: G. a Waesbergen et E. a Weyerstraten, [16—]. From the Bequest of Lessing Rosenthal, 1868–1949

Battista Guarini. *Il Pastor fido.* Amsterdam: Jodoco Pluymer, 1663.

Battista Guarini. *Il Pastor fido: Le berger fidele.* Paris: Estienne Loyson, 1676.

Battista Guarini. *Il Pastor fido: The Faithful Shepherd.* London: Printed for Henry Herringman, 1676. From the Library of George Williamson

Battista Guarini. *Il Pastor fido.* Amsterdam: S. D. Elsevier, 1678.

Jean Millet (fl. 1660). *Pastorale et tragi-comedie de Janin.* New ed., rev. and corr. Lyon: Antoine Molin, [1706].

Jean-Baptiste Molière (1622–1673). *Tartuffe: Or the French Puritan. A Comedy.* London: Printed by H. L. and R. B. for James Magnus, 1670.

François Passerat (fl. 1695). *Amarillis, petite pastoralle.* Brussels: George de Backer, 1695. Given by his Friends in Memory of Bernard Weinberg

Jacopo Sannazaro (1458–1530). *Arcadia.* Venice: [Bartholomeo ditto l'Imperadore], 1548. From the Bequest of Professor Bernard Weinberg

Elkanah Settle (1648–1724). *Pastor Fido: Or, The Faithful Shepherd. A Pastoral.* London: Printed for William Cademan, 1677.

William Shakespeare (1564–1616). *The History of King Lear.* Revived with alterations by Nahum Tate. London: Rich. Wellington, E. Rumbaud, Tho. Osborne, [1702?].

William Shakespeare. *The Works.* Rev. and corr. by N[icholas] Rowe. Vol. 2. London: Printed for Jacob Tonson, 1709.

William Shakespeare. *The Works.* Coll. and corr. by [Alexander] Pope. Vol. 1. London: Printed for Jacob Tonson, 1725.

William Shakespeare. *The Beauties of Shakespear.* 2nd ed., enl. by William Dodd. Vol. 2. London: Printed for T. Waller, 1757. Celia and Delia Austrian Study Collection

Florizel and Perdita. A Dramatic Pastoral, In Three Acts. Alter'd from *The Winter's Tale* of Shakespear by David Garrick. London: J. and R. Tonson, 1758.

William Shakespeare. *Mr. William Shakespear's Comedies, Histories, and Tragedies.* London: Methuen, 1904. Facsimile of the 1685 (fourth folio) edition.

Voltaire (1694–1778). *Lettres écrites de Londres: Sur les anglois et autres sujets.* London [i.e. Basel: Jean Brandmuller], 1737.

William Wycherley (1640–1716). *The Plain-dealer: A Comedy.* London: James Magnes, Richard Bentley, 1678.

Crossing Genres: Popular Theater, Parody & Critique

Evaristo Gherardi (d. 1700). *Le Theatre italien.* Vol. 1. Paris: Heritiers de Mabre-Cramoisy, 1695.

Alain René Le Sage (1668–1747). *Le Theatre de la foire, ou l'opera comique.* Vols. 1–3. Paris: Pierre Gandouin, 1737. The Helen and Ruth Regenstein Collection of Rare Books

Jean-Baptiste Molière (1622–1673). *Les Oeuvres.* Rev., corr., and augm. Vol. 2. Paris: Denys Thierry, Claude Barbin, Pierre Trabouillet, 1682. Gift of Julius Rosenwald

Les Parodies du nouveau theatre italien. Vols. 1, 3–4. Paris: Briasson, 1732.

Théâtre des boulevards, ou Recueil de parades. Vol. 1. Mahon [i.e. Paris]: Gilles Langlois, 1756.

II. THE RISE OF DRAMA CRITICISM

Theoretical Treatises & Critical Essays

Aristotle (384–322 B.C.E.). *La Poetica.* Vienna: Gaspar Stainhofer, 1570.

Aristotle. *Poetica.* Basel: Pietro de Sedabonis, 1576.

Aristotle. *La Poëtique.* Trans. by André Dacier (1651–1722). Paris: Claude Barbin, 1692. From the Bequest of Professor Bernard Weinberg

François Hédelin, abbé d'Aubignac (1604–1671). *La Pratique du theatre.* Paris: Denys Thierry, 1669.

François Hédelin, abbé d'Aubignac. *La Pratique du theatre.* Vol. 3. Amsterdam: Jean Frederic Bernard, 1715. From the Bequest of Professor Bernard Weinberg

Nicolas Boileau Despréaux (1636–1711). *Oeuvres.*

New ed., rev., corr., and augm. Vols. 1–2. Amsterdam: David Mortier, 1718.

John Dryden (1631–1700). *Of Dramatick Poesie, An Essay.* London: Printed for Henry Herringman, 1684.

Daniel Heinsius (1580–1655). *De tragoediæ constitutione liber.* Leiden: Ex Officinâ Elsevirianâ, 1643. From the Bequest of Professor Bernard Weinberg

Saint-Evremond (1613–1703). *The Works.* Vol. 1. London: J. and J. Knapton [et al.], 1728. From the Library of George Williamson

Giulio Cesare Scaligero (1484–1558). *Poetices libri septem.* n.p.: Petrus Santandreanus, 1581. From the Bequest of Bernard Weinberg

Lope de Vega (1562–1635). *Rimas.* Madrid: Alonso Martin, 1609. New York: DeVinne Press, 1903. Gift of Archer M. Huntington

Letters & Periodicals

Le Mercure galant. Vol. 1. Paris: Claude Barbin, after the 1673 Paris edition.

Marie de Rabutin-Chantal, marquise de Sévigné (1626–1696). *Letters of Madame de Sévigné to Her Daughter and Her Friends.* Enl. ed. Vol. 2. London: Printed for J. Walker [et al.], 1811. From the Library of Francis Hooper

Les Spectacles de Paris. Pt. 25. Paris: La veuve Duchesne, 1776.

The Spectator. Nos. 1–555. London: Printed for S. Buckley, 1711–12.

Religious Criticism

M. (Edme) Boursault (1638–1701). *Pieces de theatre.* Paris: Jean Guignard, 1695. Purchased from a Fund given in Honor of Herman H. Fussler by Bernard Weinberg

M. (Edme) Boursault. *Esope à la cour et Esope à la ville: deux comedies.* Paris: Geoffroi Lesch, 1720. Given by his Friends in Memory of Bernard Weinberg

Jeremy Collier (1650–1726). *A Short View of the Immorality and Profaneness of the English Stage.* 2d. ed. London: Printed for S. Keble, R. Sare, H. Hindmarsh, 1698.

Jeremy Collier. *A Defence of the Short View of the Profaneness and Immorality of the English Stage.* London: Printed for S. Keble, R. Sare, H. Hindmarsh, 1699.

William Congreve (1670–1729). *The Way of the World, A Comedy.* London: Printed for Jacob Tonson, 1700.

Armand de Bourbon, prince de Conti (1629–1666). *Traité de la comedie et des spectacles.* Paris: Louis Billaine, 1669.

The Stage Acquitted. Being A Full Answer to Mr. Collier, and the Other Enemies of the Drama. London: John Barnes, 1699. Berlin Collection

III.
ILLUSTRATING
THEATER

Frontispieces: Sets or Setting?

Pierre Corneille (1606–1684). *Le Theatre.* Vol. 2. Rouen: [L. Maurry], 1664.

Pierre Corneille. *Le Theatre.* Vol. 4. Paris: Guillaume de Luyne, 1666.

Pierre Corneille. *Horace, A French Tragedy.* Ed. by Charles Cotton. London: Printed for Henry Brome, 1671.

Pierre Corneille. *The Cid: or, The Heroick Daughter. A Tragedy.* London: Printed for J. W., 1714.

Battista Guarini (1538–1612). *Il Pastor fido.* Venice: Gio. B. Ciotti, 1602.

Jean-Baptiste Molière (1622–1673). *Le Misantrope, comedie.* Paris: Jean Ribou, 1667. The Helen and Ruth Regenstein Collection of Rare Books

Jean-Baptiste Molière. *Les Oeuvres.* New ed. Vols. 2, 6. Amsterdam: Henri Wetstein, 1691. Gift of Julius Rosenwald

Jean-Baptiste Molière. *Les Oeuvres posthumes.* Vol. 8. Lyon: Jacques Lions, [1696?]. From the Bequest of Professor Bernard Weinberg

Jean-Baptiste Molière. *Les Œuvres.* Rev., corr., and augm. Vol. 1. Paris: Denys Thierry, Claude Barbin, et Pierre Trabouillet, 1697.

Jean-Baptiste Molière. *De Listige Vryster, óf de verschalkte voogd; blyspél.* Amsterdam: J. Lescaille, 1707.

Perspective & Italian Set Design

Andrea Pozzo (1642–1709). *Rules and Examples of Perspective, Proper for Painters and Architects.* London: Printed by Benjamin Motte, 1707.

Sebastiano Serlio (1475–1554). *Tutte l'opere d' ar-*

chitettura. Venice: Francesco de' Franceschi Senese, 1584.

Giacomo da Vignola (1507–1583). *Le Due Regole della prospettiva pratica.* Rome: Francesco Zannetti, 1583.

Vitruvius Pollio (fl. 1st century B.C.E.). *Di Lucio Vitruuio Pollione de architectura libri dece.* [Como]: Gotardus de Ponte, [1521].

Vitruvius Pollio. *Les Dix Livres d'architecture de Vitruve.* 2nd ed., rev., cor., and augm. by Claude Perrault (1628–1703). Paris: Jean Baptiste Coignard, 1684. Berlin Collection

The Baroque Pageant

Ottaviano Castelli (d,. 1642). *La Sincerita trionfante, overo l' Erculeo ardire.* Rome: Vitale Mascardi, 1640. The Helen and Ruth Regenstein Collection of Rare Books

William D'Avenant (1606–1668). *The Works.* London: Printed by T. N. for Henry Herringman, 1673.

Inigo Jones (1573–1652). *The Designs.* [London]: William Kent, 1727.

Inigo Jones. *Festival Designs.* Exh. cat. with intro. by Roy Strong. [n.p.: Meridian Gravure, 1967?]. From the Library's General Collection

Ben Jonson (1573?–1637). *The Workes.* London: Will Stansby, 1616. The Frederic Ives Carpenter Memorial Collection

Bernard de Montfaucon (1655–1741). *Les Monumens de la monarchie françoise.* Vol. 5. Paris: Julien-Michel Gandouin, Pierre-François Giffart, 1733.

Allardyce Nicoll (1894–1976). *Stuart Masques and the Renaissance Stage.* New York: Harcourt, Brace, 1938. From the Library's General Collection

Charles Perrault (1628–1703). *Festiva ad capita annulumque decursio.* Paris: Typographia Regia, 1670. From the Library of Sir Shane Leslie, Presented by Louis H. Silver

Roma festeggiante nel Monte Pincio. [Venice: Padre Maestro Coronelli, 1687?]. The Helen and Ruth Regenstein Collection of Rare Books